Remembering Rosie

Memories of a Wisconsin Farm Girl

Nadine A. Block

PAGE PUBLISHING, INC.
Conneaut Lake, PA

First originally published by Page Publishing 2021

ISBN 978-1-6624-3050-3 (pbk)
ISBN 978-1-6624-3043-5 (digital)

Printed in the United States of America

CONTENTS

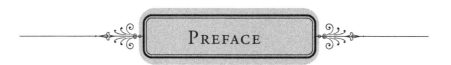

PREFACE

I grew up on a dairy farm in north-central Wisconsin in the mid-1900s. It's where my brothers and sisters and I learned to respect hard work, teamwork, and nature. Back then, 50 percent of the country's population was rural. Small family farms were abundant, and agricultural communities thrived. It was a safe place where few people locked their doors. Some didn't even own a door key. And while we didn't have much money, we never went hungry. Most of the food served on our dining room table was grown in our garden or raised in our barn. Life was simple. Everything revolved around school, church, and community. There was little contact with the outside world.

Like other farm children, my four siblings and I helped with the family business. School and chores filled our days. Downtime didn't happen often, but when it did, our property turned from a strenuous workplace into a vast playground. The rolling acres gave us plenty of room for impromptu ball games, war games, and tag. Corn and hay fields were perfect for hide-and-seek; the small stream across the road from our house was ideal for splashing one another and looking for fish; and our barn's haymow allowed us to leap from high above into piles of loose hay. Freedom was abundant. Farm parents didn't have time to hover, nor did they have any inclination to tell kids how to amuse themselves. And smartphones with apps to track kids' whereabouts were a long way off.

My parents and some of my generation lived through the Great Depression that lasted from 1929 to 1939. The Wall Street crash in 1929 had an immense effect on the country. What followed was the worst economic downturn in history. Millions of people were out of work and depended on breadlines for their survival. Radio programs talked about a worldwide depression and people lining up outside employment agencies, hoping to find work. We sympathized with people who were struggling, but living on the farm kept us insulated from hardship. Those dark days left lasting memories about the fragility of our financial system. That's when we learned frugality and started saving our money.

I was five years old when the US entered World War II. I can recall when China turned communist and Russia became our sworn enemy. At a tender age, I understood the threat of nuclear warfare was real. Once school administrators became aware that nukes were a-push-of-a-button away, they made students practice taking cover from an invincible bomb under flimsy desks. It seemed a futile exercise to me even back then.

Unlike today, no one had computers or smartphones with access to social media feeds filled with news or Google at their fingertips to find answers. As the last generation to grow up without television, we kept up-to-date listening to radio broadcasts. Edward R. Murrow, Gabriel Heatter, and President Roosevelt's fireside chats kept us in the know about our uncertain world.

After World War II, the number of small family farms in our area declined. Prosperity and the lure of an easier, more exciting life in the city led to an exodus of young adults. Between 1950 and 1970, half of the family farms in the United States had disappeared. The number of people living on farms fell from twenty million to ten million. Losses have continued. Between 2017 and 2019, over 1,600 Wisconsin dairy farms closed operations. Farmers' incomes have remained stagnant or dropped, and young people continue to leave dairy farming because the cost of machinery, seed, and food for animals have risen. Farmer suicide rates have spiked, and many farm communities have fallen apart. Country schools and stores have closed, and factory farms have taken over vast swaths of land once occupied by small farms. Empty barns and abandoned houses stand like skeletal remains of a bygone era.

Yet despite their hard lives and the future of farming, my parents expected us to remain in the country or move to a nearby town after high school graduation. Moving to a metropolitan area like Milwaukee or Minneapolis was as far away as our parents envisioned for their children. What my parents didn't realize was that the children they raised were restless. Many times, my siblings and I would be in the middle of a chore, and we'd look at one another and mutter, "There has to be an easier way to make a living." We knew there were more interesting places. We could hear the slow, deep chug of the locomotive and train whistles blowing in the distance. We knew the massive steel machine was heading to a more exciting place, and we wanted to be on board.

It's funny how we now look back in nostalgia about a place we couldn't wait to leave.

CHAPTER I

Rosie Goes to the Glue Factory

Dad told me Rosie was going to be picked up that day. I shuddered. He meant she was going to the glue factory or a slaughterhouse where she would be butchered for hamburger or pet food. The glue factory was a place where animal hooves were made into glue. I didn't want to know where Rosie was going. I was ten years old, and Rosie was my favorite cow. I balefully watched as Dad prodded her onto the ramp of the truck and as the driver, standing in the truck, pulled her up the ramp with a rope around her neck. She looked anxious and fearful. Her head jerked up and down as she struggled against the rope. Her tongue was hanging out, and saliva dripped from her mouth. She looked at me and mooed mournfully as she stumbled up the incline. She was begging not to be sent to her death. Desperately, I looked away. I couldn't save her. The driver slammed the truck's back door, and Rosie disappeared. I watched him drive down our driveway and broke into tears. I ran into the house, crawled under my bed, and sobbed.

Dad came to find me. "Come to the barn to see the new calf," he said. I stopped crying and crawled from under my bed, but I didn't respond. I had plenty of thoughts. I was mostly sad, but I was also angry. The new calf was no substitute for Rosie! The killing of Rosie was the saddest event of my childhood.

Rosie was a light-brown-and-white Guernsey cow. We were born in the same year, so we grew up together. She had limpid eyes, beautiful long eyelashes, and a long tongue that was rough to touch. She would walk with queenly grace from the pasture to her first stanchion position in the barn. Her milk was gold and creamy, and her brown hide with white patches was perfect for petting. She looked like Elsie, the mascot for the Borden Dairy Company, and I loved her.

Living on a farm gave us plenty of experience in caring for animals. It was usually fun. We fed calves, cows, pigs, chickens, Pixie the horse, and barn cats. They loved seeing us because we brought their food. It was also sad being around them because their lives were short and often cruel. Cows died from eating barbed wire fencing that sometimes got mixed up in their hay. They died giving birth or from diseases. Even though cows can live to be twenty years old, many were removed from the herd and shipped off to the glue factory or slaughterhouse and replaced by younger cows when they no longer produced milk in the quantities

Dad expected. They were usually around ten years old, just like Rosie.

She was gone forever. As a child, I had torn feelings about growing up on a farm. On that day, the bad feelings won. I vowed I would never be a farmer. I would never be a farmer's wife. I would grow up and make a life for myself where work wasn't so hard and I didn't have to participate in killing animals.

CHAPTER 2

October 7, 1936—the Firstborn

I was born as a fourth-generation Wisconsin farm girl. Or was I a boy? My mother, Sarah Ludwig, told me my birth story.

A breeze ruffled the curtains in the small bedroom on that cool, sunny October day where the twenty-year-old newlywed laid in her bed. Outside her window was forty acres of farmland that surrounded the white wood-framed house, and in the distance, a red barn and well-kept outbuildings dotted the Wisconsin landscape. In the middle of nowhere, my mother waited for the doctor who would help with the birth of her first child. As the pain in her abdomen increased, my father, twenty-one-year-old Franklin, and his parents, Anna and Anton Ludwig, dug potatoes in the field next to the house. Dad or his mother took turns checking on Mom or keeping her company.

Back then, 50 percent of women gave birth at home even though it was dangerous. Childbirth infections and childhood illnesses could easily become fatal. Unsterilized conditions, overuse of drugs, little prenatal care, and undertrained physicians often led to childbirth fatalities. Antibiotics had been discovered but were not in general use. Mothers were told babies should have sixteen hours of sleep, and they shouldn't let outsiders kiss them. Doctors warned against spoiling children. They said they shouldn't be picked up unless they were sick. Crying was good exercise for the lungs.

The doctor and his driver finally arrived. Mom remembered, "The driver was the most helpful person in your birth." He administered twilight anesthesia, which gave some relief from pain and erased memory of childbirth pain. Soon after they began their ministrations, I, Nadine Ann Ludwig, was born.

I didn't cry much. I was a happy child, a blue-eyed plump blond baby. I smiled a lot. I entertained myself; I could sit for a long time and play with toys and pots and pans. I didn't walk until I was more than a year old. Mom said, "You were a nice, obedient child, but you later turned mischievous." I didn't know what she meant. "Sassy," my sister Barbara explained to me later.

Nadine with her Dad, Franklin Ludwig

It wasn't until my mother was in her nineties that I heard my birth story. I learned that there were family murmurings that the doctors were drinkers, which may explain why he recorded my gender as male on my birth certificate, an error that I didn't realize until 2009 when I was in my late sixties. Although I've submitted my birth certificate two or three times for various reasons, I never read it. It seems no one else did either—not for my passport, not for my driver's license, and not for my marriage license. Mom and Dad probably didn't know that their little blond-haired child was described as a male. Record-keeping wasn't great in those days. It is unlikely that my parents were sent a birth certificate after my birth. Many people of my parents' age, including my mother born from immigrants, didn't even have birth certificates.

I asked her, "Didn't you ever read my birth certificate?" Her defensive response was "So didn't *you* ever read it?" She was right. It surprised and amused me, so I decided there was no need to change it.

Three Oldest Ludwig Children: Barbara, Nadine and David

She went on to have four more live births, the later ones in the Medford or Marshfield Hospital. All the children survived and are from sixty-five to eighty years of age. From oldest to youngest, they are Nadine (Block), Barbara (Schmidt), David Ludwig, Lynda (Long), and Lin Ludwig. None of them live on the homestead today. Mom survived until she was in the fourth month of her 102nd year. Dad lived until he was ninety-three. They had been married for seventy-two years.

CHAPTER 3

October 7, 1950—Growing Up "Country"

The Ludwig Farm, 1950

There was a distinct chill in the air and a light frost on the fields on the morning of October 7, 1950, when my dad headed out to begin his daily chores. No cars, airplanes, trains, or emergency vehicles made any noise, and no factories or automobile lights lit up the sky. The countryside was void of artificial light except for the one-bulb yard light that helped him find the barn when the moon waned or the fog covered the ground. Only nature's sounds echoed through the darkness. It was 5:30 a.m., but he was already singing Frankie Lane's "Lucky Old Sun" as he strode toward the barn. "That lucky old sun ain't got nothin' to do but roll around heaven all day," he crooned. Waking birds joined his tune as his steps broke the dark, deep silence of the early country morning. Dad, who was thirty-five at the time, was a strong, handsome, and healthy farmer who, along with Mom, owned a small Wisconsin dairy farm three miles west and two miles south of the small town of Stetsonville in north-central Wisconsin. It had been in his family for three generations.

The farm pioneered by Dad's grandparents started out with forty acres. After they married, my parents purchased an additional forty acres that adjoined the back of their property. In 1948, they began renting an eighty-acre farm across the road and purchased twenty more acres a mile away to use as a summer retreat for heifers. That brought our total acreage to 180. Fences on the homestead separated oats, corn, hay, and pastureland. From the air, it looked like a beautiful abstract painting with squares of ripe golden oats, flat gray-green grasses, brown plowed fields, and tall bright-green corn. A winter scene would have shown undulating white snowbanks, fence posts occasionally peeking out of snow, and wisps of smoke rising from scattered farmhouse chimneys into the cold, crisp gray air.

Sarah and Franklin Ludwig

Dad was a happy person who said repeatedly, "I'm a lucky guy" in spite of the austere, lonely life with few perks. He knew that he and Mom had a life far better than their parents. He grew up on the same farm where he was raising his family; but when he was a child, his parents used a team of horses to plow a ten-acre field, and his grandparents used oxen. The backbreaking process took days to complete, whereas Dad could plow the same field with his tractor in less than a day. Our family also had electricity—a luxury we'd acquired about a decade before. Hand-milking cows like what my grandfather and father did twice each day was a thing of the past. By 1950, our family used a single-bucket vacuum milk machine that drained the cows' udders. It was slow but still faster and less tedious than milking by hand.

Although Dad referred to himself as "just another poor farmer," our family never went hungry. We produced almost everything we needed to live. There was a large vegetable garden, apple trees, a potato field, and plenty of home-raised chicken, pork, and beef. We were eating free-range meat and poultry long before it was popular. Mom sewed much of the clothing she wore, as well as things for us kids. There was seldom money for extras and few purchased services, which is why farmers had to know how to repair machines and do their own property maintenance.

While Dad was at the barn, the rest of our family was still in bed, but we would be up before sunrise for morning chores. Even though it was my fourteenth birthday, I, along with my next two oldest siblings, had jobs to do, and Mom always watched to make sure everyone worked. My ten-year-old brother, David, would go to the barn to feed the calves. I didn't do that anymore, not since Rosie got taken away. I didn't want to get attached to the little calves. My twelve-year-old sister, Barbara, and I helped Mom. We made the beds, helped prepare a breakfast of oatmeal and fried eggs and toast, and assisted with our baby sister. When we heard crying coming from one-year-old baby Lynda's crib, we rushed to pick her up. As soon as we'd reach her crib, the crying would stop, and she'd sop up our attention. We treated our round-faced, jolly sister like a baby doll; we changed her diapers, fed her, and played with her. We felt responsible for her care because Mom often seemed over-worked and unhappy, quiet, and unsmiling.

Barbara and I made sandwiches of leftover meat from the previous night's dinner for our school lunches. We made a good team. I made the sandwiches with Mom's homemade bread, and Barbara wrapped them in wax paper and packed them in recycled syrup containers that we used for lunch buckets. Sometimes we'd include an apple from our apple trees or a home-baked sugar cookie.

I recall that morning being quiet. Barbara and I bickered about clothes. We kept our squabbles at a whispered level. "You always take the best 'our clothes' [clothes we shared]," she hissed. I sassed back, "Too bad you don't get up earlier. You could get them." I made a mental note that she would remember that. I would have to get my clothes out the night before from now on and hide them. There was a squabble or two about who took the most cookies or didn't do their fair share of work. Another protest was accompanied by knocking at the bathroom door. "Stop hogging the bathroom!" On another day, Mom might have ordered a new round of tasks for the offenders, but today she was quiet and chose to ignore the bickering.

A bottle of cod-liver oil stood on our kitchen counter. Mom believed it kept children from getting sick and administered a spoonful to us before school each day. On occasion, we'd get a quarter of an orange to chase away the bitter, oily, fishy taste. Years later, studies showed that the offensive elixir contained vitamins A and D, which help children avoid colds and flu. Apparently, mother did know best.

Barbara and David left for school by eight o'clock. They walked a mile and a half to Lawndale Elementary, but in the winter, sometimes they were lucky enough to catch a ride with a milk truck that had an attached plow. I, on the other hand, had to catch a school bus a half hour earlier to get to Medford High School. My ten-mile journey with lots of stops took an excruciating hour.

After we were off to school, Mom's day consisted of cooking, cleaning, washing clothes, hanging them on the clotheslines, and caring for Lynda. It was a lot of work, but she felt fortunate. She remembered that her mother hand-washed clothes with homemade soap and a washboard, and when my parents were first married, they didn't have electricity or indoor plumbing. Now she enjoyed conveniences like indoor plumbing, an electric washing machine, and a Kelvinator refrigerator.

We all arrived home from school between 4:00 p.m. and 5:30 p.m., and my sister and I would immediately begin our chores. We'd bring the laundry in from outside, fold it and put it away, help with dinner, and keep Lynda entertained. Dinner was served before Dad and David left to bring the cows from the field, milk them, and feed the new calves and other barn animals.

After the evening work was complete, my family—including Grandpa Anton and Grandma Anna—gathered to celebrate my fourteenth birthday. This year, Mom made a double-decker yellow cake with creamy vanilla butter frosting and served it with spumoni ice cream. The cake and ice cream all but disappeared soon after the happy birthday tune. Only two pieces were left for Barbara and David's lunch the next day. I had no leftover birthday cake, but that was okay. Sweets were not my favorite food.

My present from my grandparents was an envelope with a dollar. I was thrilled! "Wow," I said. "How great this is! I have to babysit for four hours to make this much money." My mason jar bank had almost enough money for the sweater I saw in the Sears, Roebuck and Company catalog that I was saving for. That night, I put my dollar in the jar, closed the lid, and put it under my bed. By nine o'clock, my fourteenth birthday was wrapped up, and the lights were out on the farm.

CHAPTER 4

Wisconsin Pioneers—the Fritsche Homestead

Joseph Fritsche, Wisconsin Pioneer

The history of our family in the US began with the Fritsche Homestead in 1883. In my childhood, that north-central Wisconsin acreage was called the Ludwig Farm.

It's a wonder to me why my ancestors chose to leave Germany and settle in an untamed country they knew little about with a sometimes-unforgiving climate. Wisconsin is cold. The winters are long, and the growing season is short. Wisconsinites joke that driving is better in the winter because snow fills the potholes and snowblowers get more miles than cars. "You know you're from Wisconsin if you use a snowblower on your roof" is another Badger joke.

Aside from the often-brutal weather, the pioneers also had to learn a new language. Their children would grow up speaking English and probably forget the German language and traditions. Their economic needs overcame their worries. Many of them were squeezed into tiny farms that couldn't support their families. It's likely they were eager to start somewhere new. It's hard for me to imagine how they did any serious investigation into the suitability of Wisconsin. Perhaps they corresponded with people already living in America or read glowing ads in German newspapers placed by US railroads touting the graces of farming in Wisconsin. I envision photos with farmers showing off gigantic produce with headlines screaming, "Potatoes the size of a newborn!" Most likely, the Fritsche and Ludwig families wanted more land, and the cold winters and fertile soil of Wisconsin reminded them of Austria. Plus they could afford land in Wisconsin. Land was cheap—three dollars an acre or less.

"America's Dairyland" and "Cheese Capital of the United States" would not describe Wisconsin for dozens of years. Much of Wisconsin was uncultivated and was ripe for immigrants. The best farmland was in the southern part of the state. That was no longer available. But in 1873, the Wisconsin Central Railroad built a line that ran through Central Wisconsin, Stetsonville, Medford, Whittlesey, Chelsea, and Westboro in the north. To encourage building the railroad, the US government gave the railroad company half of the cutover land, with acreage already logged out in odd-numbered sections. So aside from earning money in transporting farm goods, the railroad made even more money selling the rocky, stump-filled terrain to people like my ancestors who were looking for a fresh start.

During the German migration that took place from 1830 through the 1880s, my paternal great-grandparents joined twenty-eight other family members and came to the United States by ship from Konighs Wald, Austria. My great-grandfather, Joseph Fritsche, a widower, had three small children when he married Veronica Peissig from Tyssa, Austria, in 1880. She—along with her father, Franz Peissig, and the entire Franz Peissig family—Joseph Fritsche's three children, his mother, and his only sister were part of the group who came to Wisconsin. Joseph and Veronica built the Fritsche Homestead in Little Black Township, Taylor County, and went on to have four more children: Josie, Herman, Rudolph, and my grandmother, Anna. They were the first generation of Fritsches born in the United States.

March 3, 1883, marks the day that my great-grandparents began building a new life on forty acres of tree stump and rock-filled uncultivated land. It was five miles from the nearest small town and ten miles from the largest town and Taylor County seat, Medford; and their only means of transportation was walking or riding horses. Once they cleared some of their newly purchased land of tree stumps and rocks, they built a small, primitive house. It was one of nineteen homesteads in Little Black Township before 1900. It was probably made of logs and with clay and leaves stuffed between the timbers to keep the wind from blowing through. It had a dirt floor, which worked best since it's likely they shared the house with farm animals the first year or two. Between the stumps, they planted corn, beans, and potatoes. It's likely they had a few chickens, some pigs, and maybe a cow and a calf. Photos of pioneer farms show roughly built, unpainted homes with few windows and surrounded by tree stumps. It's a stark contrast to the large two-story, nine-room house of my childhood three generations later. Lilacs, hollyhocks, daisies, and peonies surrounded our white black-roofed house that sat on a well-kept lawn.

In 1883, Medford had two newspapers, four churches (Catholic, Methodist, Episcopal, and German Lutheran), and general merchandise stores for groceries, medicine, paints, oils, and meat. There were blacksmith shops, an attorney's office, two doctors, and four hotels. It seems unlikely though that my ancestors visited Medford often since they traveled by horse or by feet. The small towns of Dorchester and Stetsonville were closer and had small grocery stores and feed mills.

Joseph was a short, stocky, balding man with a mustache; and Veronica was a hefty, plain woman with salt-and-pepper hair that she wore drawn back in a severe bun. Photos don't show them smiling, but I suspect happiness was difficult to come by because life was so hard. In those days, entire families worked in the fields—men and women, young and old—until they grew too weak or too sick to work. It's only then that their children would care for them.

Oxen and horses did most of the heavy work. Animals pulled out tree roots to make arable land, and the family cut down trees left by loggers with handsaws and axes. However, my maternal grandfather, George Milles, preferred a more dramatic approach to clearing land. *Kaboom!* Dynamite. Despite not being able to see well or read English, George blew the roots from the earth using dynamite. After stacking the extracted roots in piles, he'd set them ablaze.

With all the backbreaking work in a rugged climate, it's no wonder Joseph Fritsche told my father, "I wish I could have taken the family back to Austria after the first few years we were here." Even with the long hours of hard labor, farmers had to supplement their income by working in lumber mills to put food on the table. Thankfully, food prices were cheap in the mid-to-late-1800s. Coffee was eleven cents a pound, and you could get eight bars of soap for a quarter. You could even get a set of false teeth for ten dollars.

Joseph Fritsche died on March 4, 1926, on the homestead. Dad remembers being eleven years old and coming home from school to find his grandfather dead. "He was laid out on the dining room table, which was covered with a black cloth. There were dimes on his eyelids," Dad said. Joseph was described in his obituary as "a good Christian and pioneer farmer." Veronica Fritsche died on October 15, 1935. She had been in declining health for years with what Dad said was "dropsy," edema caused by congestive heart failure. Like her husband, she died on the homestead.

The Fritsche children all married and stayed in Wisconsin. Herman and Rudolph farmed and lived within five miles of the homestead. Josie lived with her husband, Dennis Murphy, in Madison, Wisconsin. Anna, my paternal grandmother, remained on the homestead after marrying my grandfather, Anton Ludwig.

My paternal grandfather, Anton Ludwig, was born in Prezbendow, Galicia (Austrian Empire), on November 7, 1878. He immigrated with his parents, Frank and Marianne Andersch Ludwig, in 1882. They came from Wiesenthal, which is a village now called Lucany in the

Czech Republic. Their month-long journey to a new life was aboard a steamship, the *British Queen*, steerage class. After coming to Wisconsin, Anton met Anna, and they married on June 19, 1906. By 1913, Anna and Anton Ludwig had purchased the farm from Anna's parents who moved to Stetsonville. Anton was active in the community and worked as an auctioneer in farm sales. Anna and Anton lived and worked on the family farm until 1937 when they sold it to my parents. When my grandparents left the farm, they retired to a small house in Stetsonville as what the Fritsches had done. They lived on Social Security checks, which became available that year, income from the sale of the farm, and my grandfather's wages from the Stetsonville feed mill where he worked for fifteen of his retirement years. They lived frugally. Grandpa called anyone who walked out of an empty room without turning off the lights wasteful. I smile as I always turn off the lights when I leave a room. I learned my lesson well.

On Sundays after church, we would visit my grandparents. My grandmother, Anna, was a quiet, plump woman with bright blue eyes who loved handing out cookies to her grandchildren, and sometimes, to our delight, she gave us quarters. While the grown-ups chatted, I sometimes wandered into the dining room, where my grandparents would often play Schafskopf or "Sheep's Head" cards or Cribbage with friends. I would try and face my fear of Grandpa Anton's hunting treasure. It was a large deer head with sharp antlers and spooky black eyes made of glass. I was certain that the woodland creature hanging on the wall was staring right at me. I tried to push away my aversion by imagining throwing hoops over his antlers.

Grandma Anna died on February 5, 1968, having suffered for years from cancer. Grandpa Anton was found dead on the kitchen floor five days later, February 10, 1968. Dad said his father died of old age. "His heart was no bigger than a walnut."

CHAPTER 5

Beer, Bratwurst, and Building a Community

German settlers brought hot dogs, potato salad, beer, and polkas to America. We can also thank them for Christmas trees and fairy tales like *Struwwelpeter* by Heinrich Hoffman. It's an 1845 collection of morality tales where men with giant scissors humiliate and mutilate children. Thankfully, I don't recall being read any bedtime tales about children being tortured and killed for their stupidity, misbehavior, and bad manners. When I read *Struwwelpeter* as an adult, it gave me chills.

Despite their sometimes-ghastly folklore, Germans were civic-minded people who came to America to make life better. By 1900, thirty-four percent of the over two million people living in Wisconsin, 709,909, were of German background. They heavily influenced Wisconsin culture. German immigrants liked living among one another and enjoyed social activities. They joined educational and cultural organizations like music and athletic groups, and they initiated farmer cooperatives. My dad served as a director on co-ops like cheese factories and stores serving our community. He also served on the REA (Rural Electric Association) Board of Directors from 1971 through 1977 and the school board of our one-room rural school for years. He was an example of civic-minded German immigrants.

Dad was the treasurer and tax collector for our town of Little Black for twenty years. I cherished sitting with him at the dining room table and helping him calculate tax bills. As Dad read the valuations and multipliers, I typed them into a mechanical calculator called an adding machine. I felt important when I'd crank the handle to find the totals. My brothers and sisters helped when they were old enough, and of course, Dad would always check our work. Even though he wasn't one to dole out much praise, we felt rewarded that he trusted us enough to let us assist.

Taylor County is home to the oldest Old Order Amish community in Wisconsin, and it's made up of families with last names like Yoder, Troyer, Hochstetler, and Beiler. The Amish lived without the aid of cars, telephones, tractors, or electricity. If they bought a farm with power lines, they'd rip them out. Even education was simplified. Amish schooling ended after the eighth grade so kids could focus on a trade or farming and not be swayed into a life removed from their faith. In 1972, the Supreme Court ruling on *Wisconsin v.*

Yoder agreed that it was their right to stop formal education past eighth grade. But like the rest of Wisconsin, the Amish still paid taxes. I remember the serious, devout men with black clothes and long beards pulling up to our house in horse-drawn carriages. The Amish men would sit with Dad at the kitchen table and pay their taxes in cash.

One day after the buggy pulled away, I saw Dad leave out the back door with an envelope of money. "What are you going to do with that?" I asked. "Come. I'll show you my bank," he said as he headed for a couple of trees next to the clotheslines. Dad hid the money he collected in a hole in the old willow tree in our backyard until he could get to the bank. After years of being treasurer and stashing money in a tree, Dad wanted to step down from his position. He found a willing candidate to run for the job, and he worked hard to get him elected. But when the results came in, Dad found the job was still his. Folks elected him as a write-in candidate, so he reluctantly did it for a few more years.

Our area of Wisconsin was reputed to be 90 percent German Catholic, but there were also Lutheran Swedes, who, like Norwegian and German immigrants, were mostly middle-class and came to the US because they liked Wisconsin's climate and soil. Scandinavians and Germans lacked arable land in their home countries and could find it in Wisconsin. Like Germans, Scandinavians incorporated their traditions and skills to American life. They had common interests in education, environmental concerns, equality, and a desire to improve the community. They were political and advocated for their concerns. They tended to be frugal, putting their money in more land or crops. They worked patiently, slowly, and methodically to better themselves.

The Scandinavians and Germans had an antagonistic but friendly relationship. The Germans told jokes that made fun of a supposed lack of Swedish intelligence, and the Swedes made jokes about the purported stubbornness of Germans. Wisconsin German expats like to tell these jokes, as I do, and we enthusiastically imitate the Scandinavian accent, although not very well. While Ole and Lena were jokes about Norwegians, we usually attributed them to be Swedish like our neighbors. The jokes usually start with "Have you heard this one about Ole and Lena?

"Just Married" is a typical Ole and Lena Joke:

Ole and Lena got married. On their honeymoon trip, they were nearing Minneapolis when Ole put his hand on Lena's knee. Giggling, Lena said, "Ole, you can go a little farder now if ya vant to." So Ole drove to Duluth.

As children, we only had a vague understanding of the comfort, security, and friendship our community gave us. If someone was ill, neighbors brought food. Everyone in town was a friend. Parties drew big crowds, and funerals were always well attended. They were like another aspect of our social life. A wind chill temperature of minus thirty degrees that December day in 2009 did not deter people from attending Dad's funeral. Over one hundred people in our town of fewer than a thousand showed up. I delivered a eulogy for Dad and looked down at the gathering, almost all elderly, with canes and wheelchairs, who came despite strong winds, freezing temperatures, and snowdrifts. *What hardy folks*, I thought. The funeral home decided not to bury Dad's ashes until it warmed up. In past generations, before cremation, he might have been put in the granary until spring when the ground began thawing.

But even with all the advantages of this tight-knit community, there were some drawbacks. It bred a narrowness of ideas and what behavior was acceptable. Outsiders included anyone not white, Christian, rural, or accepting of our values. Anyone not meeting the stringent criteria was immediately noticed. Comments would begin circulating as soon as someone with a different look or religion was spotted or if someone suspected anyone was "putting on the dog" and looked or acted like they were better than others. There was also gossiping about who drank too much, who was running around on their spouse, who was beating his children, or who was PG (pregnant).

There were no faces from India, Japan, Mexico, or China, and gays were closeted. Before high school, I didn't know what being gay meant. No one was identified by others as homosexual and no one came out as such. If adults discussed this, we children were unaware.

No black or brown people lived in the community. African Americans came to Wisconsin as early as 1700, but by 1860, there were still only about twelve hundred in the state. Most were slaves of settlers. I don't recall seeing African Americans around, and their mistreatment didn't penetrate our insular lives. I do recall seeing pictures of police and dogs chasing them when I was a young adult, and public demonstrations involving racism could no longer be dismissed. I thought that people who would do that were mean but had little knowledge of or even interest in racism and race issues. There was one Jewish man who lived in our town who'd married a local gentile girl and ran a grocery store and feed mill that his father started. I remember people, including Dad, talking about "Jewing down" someone on a business deal. I don't think they even thought about what they were saying.

Dad's sister's husband ran off after a few months of marriage, so Aunt Alma moved in with her parents and worked as a grocery store clerk for most of her life. Folks gossiped about her dating in her later years because it was considered sinful. Even though she was divorced, she was still married in the eyes of the Catholic church. She was a kind woman who took care of her parents in their old age and left us kids, her nieces and nephews, small bequests when she died.

As my siblings and I grew older, we began to look at our hometown more critically.

CHAPTER 6

Ride a Horse or Walk

When my dad, Franklin, was a little boy, his family didn't have a car. Their transportation choices were walking or riding horses. He and his siblings had to walk five miles to church or the closest store. "It seemed like a heck of a long way to a kid, especially carrying groceries on our backs," Dad said. Although their farm produced most of their food, they had to buy sugar, flour, salt, baking powder, and spices.

Anton and Anna Ludwig's Car in Winter

My grandparents Anton and Anna Ludwig bought a Ford Model T in their old age, and they would reminisce about their travels, often interrupting each other to announce the exact day they left on a car trip. "May second," my grandfather said. "No, no," Grandma said. "It was May fifth." Whatever date one said, the other was sure it was a day or two later or a year or two earlier. My grandmother always gave in to my grandfather's memories, which made me cringe. Weren't her memories equally valid?

Grandpa and Grandma took a couple of memorable trips to visit relatives in southern Wisconsin. Sometimes they drove on corduroy roads, which were logs laid perpendicular to the direction of the road and spaced like railroad ties and covered with dirt. Traveling on those must have shaken dentures loose. Our country roads were unpaved, made of dirt or gravel.

During the pioneer days, there was no way to store milk from the evening and morning milking. Each day, Dad and his father delivered cans of milk with horses to the Pleasant View Co-op, the cheese factory that was a mile away. When I was growing up, we kept milk cool in cold water tanks in the milk house, a small building next to the barn. A milk truck would pick it up from the farm, weigh it, siphon it into a big tank, and take it to the cheese factory.

Many Wisconsin farmers used workhorses into the 1950s. We had a horse, Pixie, but it was too dumb and wild for farmwork. Besides, we no longer needed horses for work. We were lucky to get our first gasoline tractor before I was in school. We were probably one of the early farms in our community to have one, before 1940. And because Dad was frugal like his parents, I suspect our tractor was used. I remember always having a Farmall or a John Deere tractor—sometimes both. These were neither powerful nor comfortable. There was no cab—just a seat on an engine with four wheels and a hitch for pulling implements centered in the rear. The original price of a Farmall tractor at midcentury was 1,400 dollars, a hefty investment for a small farmer. You can get a 1955 Farmall tractor on eBay for around 2,000 dollars. A farm tractor today can cost 150,000 dollars or more.

We had fun arguing about which tractor was the best. "Allis-Chalmers is the best," my brothers said when we got one. The girls chimed in with our agreement. No matter if your family had a Farmall, an Allis-Chalmers, or a John Deere. Each child would say the brand their family owned was the best. And we all enjoyed tractor pulls at county fairs. Farmers liked to demonstrate that they had the strongest tractors. It was exciting to watch them hitch field tractors to weighted sleds, usually with big rocks, and race to see who could pull the sled the farthest with the heaviest weight in front of a huge crowd. Wisconsinites still enjoy tractor pulls at county fairs.

World War II brought about an uptick in the economic well-being for most folks, even farmers. Milk prices rose, and my dad was able to buy a brand-new car for about 1,400 dollars. My dad's happiest day was when he drove home his first new car, a Pontiac with a Hydra-Matic transmission. It was General Motors' first car with an automatic transmission, which meant we didn't have to learn to drive in a manual shift car. We took photos with excited family members standing beside the car, but no one was prouder than my dad. We had finally "arrived."

CHAPTER 7

Electricity Arrives at Last!

I looked up at the kitchen ceiling with amazement at the glowing light bulb! I stared so hard my eyes watered. I was four years old, and this was the most exciting day of my life! It was like heaven! We had electricity! I was afraid it would never come back again if we shut it off. The first thing Dad bought was a radio. We had a battery radio, but it was not dependable. An electric radio gave us a trustworthy report of what was going on in the world, and it gave us entertainment.

It's hard to imagine life without the conveniences electricity allows us. New York City had an electric power plant in the 1880s. By the 1920s, half of the urban homes in the US had electricity. But in 1930, only 13 percent of US farms had electricity. Imagine growing up without electric lighting, air-conditioning, refrigerators, washing machines, clothes dryers, electric irons, toasters, vacuum cleaners, electric sewing machines, microwave ovens, and hair dryers. Mom cooked meals on a stove that burned wood. There were no temperature settings on the stove. She had to adjust the stove vents on the firebox to get air for the fire. Before electric irons, she heated wedges of iron on the kitchen stove to use in ironing. We used the same kerosene lanterns that Mrs. O'Leary's cow kicked over, which caused the Great Chicago Fire in 1871, a story believed today to be untrue. Luckily, none of ours were ever knocked over by clumsy livestock, and the precarious lanterns left our family and farm unscathed.

Aside from the creature comforts we're accustomed to today, the lack of electricity made the workday harder and affected farmers' incomes. There were no electric saws, milk coolers, or barn cleaners. Milking cows by hand took a lot of time every morning and evening. Without the aid of electric milking machines, farmers couldn't have more than twenty cows. Milking machines allowed Dad to buy more cattle, and more cattle meant more money. Electricity made life more comfortable for the animals. When temperatures plummeted, we brought our baby chicks inside the house to keep them from freezing. Later, electricity allowed us to have heaters in the henhouse to warm the chicks and keep them safe.

A dirty coal-fired furnace provided heat for our house, but it was hard work to keep the fire burning. After the Farmer's Co-op truck unloaded the coal into a chute that dumped the black rocks into our basement, my parents or us older kids shoveled it into the fire. It was hard to keep the furnace burning, and Dad soon bought a stoker which used worm gears to push coal into the firebox at regular intervals, so we did not have to constantly fill the furnace. Later, between 1945 and 1950, we got an oil furnace.

In warm weather, we moved into our second-floor summer bedrooms that were larger and cooler. It was a glorious day when we didn't have to share small bedrooms. In the winter, we used the cold, unheated bedrooms to dry laundry that would have frozen stiff outdoors. Until we got electric fans—and later, a clothes dryer—it took days for winter laundry to dry. Since three children were born within their first six years of marriage, laundry was a cumbersome, ongoing chore. At one point before we had electricity, Dad got a second job working for a neighbor to earn money to buy a gas motor for the washing machine. The addition of a gas motor was a lifesaver in washing diapers. An electric washing machine was even better.

Until we were able to upgrade from air-drying clothing to using electric appliances, summer was greatly anticipated because we could hang wet laundry on outdoor clotheslines. Mom insisted on hanging bed linens on the outside lines with underwear and personal clothing inside. Socks had to hang toes up with clothespins. God forbid if you hung the socks upside down! "Go out and rehang them,"

Mom scolded. The sweet smell of clean laundry dried by the wind and sun still lingers in my nostrils. Artificial scents of laundry supplements cannot replicate that wholesome smell.

Unlike today where we get water from a filtered tap or plastic bottles, we got our water from a well. One well next to our barn brought water up with a twenty-foot-tall windmill that had metal blades at the top arranged in a circle like a sunflower. When the wind blew and the blades rotated, a pump rod would go up and down and, and, and cupped seals inside the long pipe brought fresh water to the surface. Twenty-five dollars would buy a beautiful wind-mill from Sears, Roebuck in 1910. We also had a well next to the house with a hand pump. We developed strong arms pumping water for home use. My parents still dreamed of indoor plumbing.

When I was a small child, most Wisconsin farmers, including my family, did not have toilets, showers, or bath-tubs. Our weekly bath meant heating water in copper boil-ers on a woodstove and filling the washtub. Bathing would begin with the youngest child and end with the oldest. By the time it was my turn, the water was cold and dirty. How lucky for me. It's no wonder that I splurge in my bathroom. My bathroom is spacious and has both a glassed-in shower and a bathtub. I love my silver and white wallpaper and the porcelain-tiled floors covered with Oriental rugs to warm my feet. I recognize the luxury of soaking in a steaming bubble bath using perfumed soaps with strawberry, lemon, or gardenia scents. It's a far cry from the medicated smell of the awful orange Lifebuoy soap we used when I was a kid.

Our toilet was a wooden rectangular two-seater that stood near the barn. The pine outhouse was lightweight and easy to move when the earthen pit filled up and needed cleaning. Unlike stereotypical images of outhouses, we did not have a star (men's toilet) or waning moon (women's toilet) cut in the door. We had enough privacy that allowed us to leave the door open for light and—even more import-ant—ventilation. And instead of soft two-ply toilet tissue, we used pages from the Sears, Roebuck or the "Monkey Ward" (Montgomery Ward) catalogs. The onetime wish-books became essential amenities. Besides, in the summer, you could sit on the toilet paging through the catalog.

Around the time I started elementary school, we got indoor plumbing, which was made possible by electricity. Hot and cold running water became a reality. Buried in the lawn outside the bathroom was a concrete box septic system that used surrounding soil in a field to filter the discharge from the septic tank. The septic tank needed to be pumped out regularly and repaired.

Dad and Mom, often during a Sunday afternoon drive, would speculate who was the boss of the family, the wife, or the husband, by the appearance of the barn or the house. If the house were large and kept up better than the barn, they'd say, "I guess the wife is the boss."

After Dad retired, I asked him what the most important advance in technology in his lifetime was. Airplanes? Cars? Without missing a beat, he said, "Electricity! I could hook an electric motor to anything and make hard work easier." Electricity was a blessing—a cleaner, safer, and more powerful blessing to everyone on our farm.

CHAPTER 8

Sarah and Franklin's Early Years

Twenty-five years ago, I took a photo of Mom and Dad when they were in their thirties to a printer for copying. At that time, printers were careful about copyrights and refused to copy professional photos. As the printer examined the image for copyright information, he asked if the people in the photo were movie stars. A smug smile came across my face, and I said, "They're my parents."

They were a handsome couple. Dad had black hair, piercing light-gray eyes, and a chiseled jaw. My son Greg favors him in looks. Mom had a pretty face and beautiful smile. Neither was blond, but there was enough light hair in the family tree that my siblings and I were almost white-haired as young children, except Lynda. Lynda favored the dark-haired ancestors, which gave my siblings and me plenty of teasing ammunition. We called her our adopted sister. We'd follow up with a "Just kidding," but I know it hurt. As an adult, she's countered us by saying, "At least I know who my father is!"

My mom was the last child born to Lithuanian immigrants George Milles and Barbara Barsdas Milles, an orphan, in 1916. Mom had four older siblings: Alex and Leona, the twins; a sister named Francis; and a brother, Pete. They were tall and nice-looking with Slavic features and light hair. My cousin found during family research interviews that Grandma Barbara was Grandpa George's second wife. She didn't like the United States and went back to Lithuania for a time.

Grandparents George and Barbara Milles, Anton and Anna Ludwig

Between 1899 and 1914, more than 250,000 Lithuanians immigrated to the United States, although they were often listed as Poles or Russians. My grandfather—born as George Millasius in Telsai, Lithuania—came to the US in 1903. Most likely, he was in search of a better life, but there were family whispers that he left to escape conscription by the czar of Russia. He was a thin quiet man over six feet tall who was hard of hearing and not fluent in English. I recall him using Lithuanian words that only Mom understood.

Grandpa George's parents bought a farm for him in Pennsylvania through a Catholic newspaper, but it turned out to be swampland. He blamed the Catholic church for his poor land and refused to attend mass. It wasn't until he was on his deathbed that Grandpa George talked to a priest.

He worked in foundries when he came to the US, and he and Grandma Barbara lived in Chicago and Rockford, Illinois, which is where my mother was born. Shortly after her birth in 1916, my grandparents moved to a small farm near Medford, Wisconsin. Mom didn't have a birth certificate, but she did have a baptismal certificate that showed her to be a year older than she claimed. According to church records, Mom was 102 when she died. Mom said the baptismal certificate was in error and always denied being older—probably because that would have made Dad younger.

She grew up poor and went hungry at times. One of the highlights of her childhood was when she and her family went to a nearby lumber camp for dinner. She spoke wistfully about the tables full of delicious food and wonderful pies.

After graduating from a small rural elementary school like Dad's, Mom went on to get her diploma from Medford High School. There were no school buses to take her to school. She showed her mettle by getting an apartment in Medford and working as a hotel housekeeper for five dollars a week during her high-school years. Most weekends, she would walk ten miles each way to visit her parents.

When she was in her eighties, I elicited Mom's childhood memories by giving her a Brandy Old Fashioned. Once the lubricating spirits loosened her tongue, I captured a family secret on my tape recorder. I learned that my quiet, shy, and reclusive Grandma Barbara who seldom spoke English was a bootlegger. They were so poor during prohibition in the 1920s and early 1930s that she took advantage of the illegal liquor trade. It's unclear whether Grandma made the corn liquor (ground corn, yeast, sugar, and water), but she distributed the spirits.

The recording of Mom's voice reminisced about walking with her mom to deliver moonshine to lumber mill workers in metal syrup pails and having revenuers visit their farm. Federal agents, prepared to enforce the Eighteenth Amendment that prohibited alcohol, poked holes in an enormous haystack, looking for the moonshine cache. They never found it.

I didn't know Grandma well even though we saw her and Grandpa often. In her old age, Grandma's mental illness that caused her to spend a short time in an institution worsened. She believed that neighbors were moving her fences. Psychiatric disorders were a hush-hush subject, so Mom didn't talk about it much.

At the end of Grandma's life, Mom took me to see her at the hospital. She looked out her window at a church steeple and said that when she was released, she wanted to go back to church. She died of liver cancer before that could happen. When Mom and Dad took us to the funeral home, an organ played gruesome dirge music. I hated it. It seemed to purposefully make people sad, and I complained to Mom, "Can't you make them stop that awful music? It is giving me a headache."

While Dad was a solid, mostly happy person, Mom was a restless, emotional person who seldom smiled. Like her mother, a model of unfulfilled dreams, she was enveloped by unhappiness and discontent for many years. We tried to please her, and I think it turned me into a sunshine fairy. I believed it was my job to flit around and make people around me happy. Sometimes I was angry with her. Couldn't she be happy and smiling like other moms? By the time I was in elementary school, I knew that I wanted to be more like Dad. He was solid and patient and gave us stability and confidence to handle whatever came our way. Mom seemed to cause turbulence in the family, and Dad tried to steady the ship by not arguing back.

Unwittingly, I kept a measure of Mom's restlessness. I wanted, as my mother seemed to want, something more exciting than farm life could offer.

Grandpa George lived with our family after Grandma died. His tall wooden chair with a reed-caned seat was in an alcove off the kitchen by windows that looked out into the backyard and barn. It was his favorite spot to smoke his corncob pipe and read his Lithuanian newspaper, *Vilnius*. It was a communist newspaper published in Chicago. Living under control of the czar probably made Lithuanians like him decide communism was better.

As teens, we knew about our homegrown right-wing Wisconsin Republican Senator Joseph McCarthy and his years of leading congressional investigations of communists supposedly infiltrating our government. He was always in the news. We groused to Mom and Dad that we would never be able to work for the government with a communist, our grandfather, in the family. We were embarrassed.

I hated the smell of Grandpa's Old Summertime tobacco. I'd produce copious fake coughs and open a window next to his chair to let the smoke outside.

He liked to pick and eat wild mushrooms that Mom would fry in butter. Mom liked them too, but because he didn't see well, she wasn't sure if he could tell which mushrooms were poisonous. I asked her if she liked them. She whispered, "I love mushrooms, but I'll wait to see if he gets sick before I try them."

Grandpa George kept a pint of something under his bed—likely schnapps—and often sang Lithuanian songs at bedtime. By the time he was in his late eighties, he developed heart problems and couldn't climb the stairs to his bedroom, so my dad carried him. Mom and Dad eventually put him in a Medford nursing home. He walked ten miles out into the country, looking for our farm, when a veterinarian found him and brought him home. He didn't go back to the nursing home, but it wasn't long before he was dying. And despite his anger toward the Catholic church, instead of turning to the wall to avoid the priest Mom brought in, he received him.

My dad was born in 1915 and grew up on the Fritsche Homestead with his older siblings Ray, Edna, and Alma. Dad and his siblings attended Lawndale Elementary, a one-room school a mile and a half west of the farm. Dad was a good student, but he didn't talk about it. According to a neighbor's son whose father attended school with dad, Dad was the smartest guy in Little Black Township, and he skipped three grades. His schooling ended after eighth grade because there were no buses to the high school that was ten miles away. At that time, only a third of Wisconsin teens graduated from high school. It seems hard to imagine being out of school forever at eleven or twelve years of age; but he was the last child at home, and his parents needed him on the farm. After he graduated from elementary school, he helped his parents and worked for his older sister Edna and her husband, Herb Voit, on their farm for two dollars a week.

CHAPTER 9

The Blind Date

"Lucille, my best friend, and her boyfriend fixed me up with a blind date with Franklin," Mom told me. "I was eighteen, and we went to a polka dance. It was out in the country, near where my parents lived. We got stuck a couple of times getting there on the muddy roads."

The dance took place in a rough, unadorned wooden building with benches along the walls and outhouses in the back. Live music poured through windows of the structure, and the sound of polkas and waltzes played by a small band. Dances were a popular form of entertainment for young Wisconsinites. They probably loved the music, or maybe it was because some young people knew someone who had access to a car. There were not a lot of choices about where to go. It was a great place for young people, like my parents, who could dance close together despite how the clergy preached about young people's sinful behavior.

My parents married on April 28, 1936, at the Holy Rosary Catholic Church in Medford, Wisconsin. It was a shotgun marriage, a colloquial term for a hurry-up wedding before an unplanned birth that seemed to embarrass Mom. I don't remember my parents celebrating or even mentioning their wedding anniversary until they were old.

Hurry-up marriages were not uncommon since the Catholic church did not permit contraception, abortions were illegal, and contraceptive methods were unreliable. When a couple got married in our community, there was often a charivari (shivaree), a late-night commotion created at the newlyweds' home with pan banging and raucous serenading by neighbors. The revelers wouldn't leave until someone handed over money that they would put to good use at a local bar.

After they married, Mom and Dad lived on the family farm with Grandpa and Grandma Ludwig. Mom didn't like sharing the house with her in-laws; and one year after I was born, my grandparents moved to town, and my parents had a mortgage. Mom believed her in-laws thought Dad could have married better, and she acted toward them according to her belief. She reluctantly invited them for dinners and family events and scowled at the mention of Dad's relatives.

"He's a menace. He'll kill someone," Mom said. Her complaints about Grandpa Anton were common since he often drove on two wheels, turning from our driveway onto the main road. She also thought he was crazy for driving forty miles to a lake, digging a hole in the ice, and sitting with a pole, trying to catch fish. "He can't even turn a corner, much less drive eighty miles," she'd rail. She couldn't find anything to like about him. Most of the time, Dad took this treatment stoically since he preferred to avoid confrontations. Mom looked for problems to worry over. She accused Dad of having a crush on or an affair with her sister-in-law. She got into tiffs with her sister, Leona, and they didn't speak for months at a time. When Leona died, Mom wasn't mentioned in her obituary even though she lived only seven miles away.

Mom wouldn't step into a store or gas station where she thought she had been slighted. She tried to make us accomplices in her grudges. She told us we shouldn't talk to someone she was on the outs with. I ignored her and thought she should fight her own battles and leave us out of it. I didn't talk back much, but I am sure she felt my disapproval.

Maybe that's what she called my "mischievous" behavior—my scowl, squinting eyes, and lockjawed silence.

CHAPTER 10

Not Much Money

Mom never forgot that she had only one dress when she started high school. Even though money was tight, she loved to buy new clothes. Dad seldom complained. She also liked home improvements. I surreptitiously accused her of being a Russian bureaucrat who put out five-year development plans like the communist government. Dad seldom turned down her requests although he often procrastinated in fulfilling them. If her demands went unheeded, she went into action. One of her remodeling ideas got its start when she knocked a hole in the kitchen wall because Dad didn't start the job promptly.

Until after high school, I knew little about the world outside Taylor County. We never flew in planes or took train rides longer than the five-mile trip on the Soo Line from Medford to Stetsonville, and the farthest we drove was to Harrisburg, Pennsylvania, to visit Mom's cousins. We didn't have a TV or a daily newspaper, and we seldom went to movies or ate in restaurants. There were not many books in our home. Our parents only read books for information, not entertainment. We did not have children's books. Even our school library was sparse. Most of our information and entertainment came from the radio and the Milwaukee Journal and the Milwaukee Sentinel Sunday newspapers.

Even with little disposable income, we didn't feel poor. We owned a prosperous farm. We lived as well or better than our neighbors. We didn't buy much prepared food like Kraft macaroni dinners, Fig Newtons, or Toll House cookies even though they were available. Dad loved spongy white store-bought bread more than home-baked loaves. I never understood that because the home-baked bread was so delicious. When I was a young housewife, I baked bread like my mom.

Prices at that time were low, but so were incomes. In 1940, the average income per year was 1,725 dollars (US Census Bureau.)

According to an online source, the People History:

In 1940, a new house cost 3,920 dollars.
In 1940, a gallon of gas was 11 cents.
In 1940, the average cost of a new car was 850 dollars.
In 1940, 100 aspirin cost 76 cents.
In 1940, a Philco refrigerator was 239 dollars.

In 1940, pork loin roast per pound was 45 cents.

In 1940, an Emerson bedroom radio was 19.65 dollars.

In 1940, men's suits were sold from 24.50 dollars.

In 1940, a portable electric heater cost 42.50 dollars.

In 1940, a Ford Super Deluxe sedan coupe was 1,395 dollars.

In 1940, a Sealy mattress cost 38 dollars.

There was no hired help on the farm. It was a twenty-four-seven job. Fathers and sons did most of the work in the field and the barn, and children learned early on that raspberries, strawberries, and blueberries didn't drop off bushes into bowls. Women worked constantly. I witnessed the saying, "A woman's work is never done." Besides having the main responsibility for rearing children, women kept large gardens and raised chickens. Money from selling eggs to the grocery store was nice pocket money for farm wives. During the busy harvest seasons, women helped the men and boys in the fields.

Mothers and daughters canned produce grown in the gardens, did laundry, cared for the house, and made meals that included baking bread, pies, doughnuts, and cakes from scratch. When I was little, Mom even made laundry soap out of lye and lard. The heated liquid was poured into molds and cut into bars when the mixture cooled. The gray-white soap was harsh and smelled awful, but it was a good cleaner. Luckily, we didn't have to use it for bathing.

I've often believed that part of Mom's unhappiness was the drudgery of her lot—the same hard work done over and over, never varying except for seasonal jobs, and with little gratitude from anyone. Who wanted to grow up to be a farmer or, God forbid, a farmer's wife? Not me.

CHAPTER 11

Leaning Left

"Franklin Roosevelt helped farmers like me. He cared about us. I don't know when, if ever, we would have gotten electricity without him," Dad said with heartfelt thankfulness. "The electric company wanted us to pay thousands of dollars to bring in power lines for electricity. We couldn't afford that." Roosevelt's New Deal Rural Electrification Act (1936) provided loans to set up cooperatives to construct power lines to bring electricity to farmers. Electric companies fought the New Deal legislation but lost. An REA office in Medford was established in 1937, and within a couple of years, we got electricity.

Our parents were lifelong democrats strongly influenced by the New Deal legislation of President Roosevelt. They identified with progressive ideology that believes the government's role is to help the little guy and blunt corporate greed. Robert La Follette passed Mom and Dad's progressive's test. He campaigned against corporate greed and introduced reforms to protect individuals. He became Wisconsin's governor in 1900. In 1906, he became a senator. In the 1930s, the Wisconsin Progressive Party was involved in developing much of Roosevelt's New Deal legislation, legislation which was meant to help the needy, provide jobs, reform banks, and speed the economic recovery from the Great Depression. My grandparents were ecstatic to receive another boon of New Deal legislation: the first round of monthly Social Security checks in 1940, referred to by Dad as "welfare checks." The Social Security Act was passed in 1935 and gave retirees of sixty-five and older a government retirement program. Our grandparents had put little into the program and were retiring or taking small part-time jobs. While checks were small, sometimes twenty or thirty dollars, it was a lot of money to them and gave them a sense of security.

Wisconsin was a progressive state prior to and throughout my parents' youth. It's been changing for decades for various reasons: fewer desirable jobs, anti-unionism popularized by conservative causes, and gerrymandering. Today, few people of moderate or poor incomes see benefits from the government. The positive attitude toward government of my childhood has been eroded by the deaths of people like Mom and Dad who lived through the Depression and saw democrats making their lives better.

In 1945, when I was nine years old, I remember hearing on the radio that President Roosevelt died. I knew this was a sad moment and ran out the back door and past the lilac trees to the yard where my parents were working. I broke the news, and they teared up like someone in the family had passed. They remained as democrats until their death. Dad didn't live to see George W. Bush out of office, his fervent wish. He lived a couple of months after Obama was elected, but he had developed dementia with Parkinson Disease, so he probably did not know.

My sister Barbara gave Mom some parting words to help ease her in dying: "You can go now. Daddy is waiting for you" and "There are lots of Chico clothing stores in heaven." She didn't think to tell our mom that Donald Trump was impeached, a little falsehood that would have made Mom happy. She thought of it on her way home from the hospital and vowed to tell her the next day. It was too late.

Dad was a tireless promoter of farming and farm products. When we came back to the farm as young adults extolling the wonders of margarine, he was visibly upset with this heresy coming from his children. "Good grief," he railed, red-faced. "Oleo is just plastic and only one molecule off motor oil. You eat that stuff?" Margarine was fake butter that was cheap to produce and was promoted by some medical sources as a healthy choice. The bagged white gelatinous substance, like Crisco, came with yellow food coloring that you kneaded into it so it looked like butter.

Dad's fight against oleo and other margarine was already being carried on by the state legislature, which wanted to protect dairy farmers. In 1895, the State Legislature passed a law prohibiting the manufacture or sale of yellow oleomargarine. The powerful farmer's lobby was afraid it would put farmers out of business because it was cheaper than butter. This law led to people smuggling oleo into Wisconsin in car trunks. It was hard to police. It remained illegal for almost seventy-five years until it was finally decriminalized in 1967. There are still butter laws. State institutions in Wisconsin like prisons, hospitals, and schools cannot substitute margarine for butter except for health reasons. Irish butter, a rich imported butter favored by butter aficionados like my husband, can't be sold in Wisconsin. Butter police are still alive and well and are laying down the butter laws in Wisconsin, but it isn't enforced much these days.

"Everything tastes better with butter," Mom said, and she was right! I got over my oleo days. In our house, we keep a quarter pound of butter in a dish on the kitchen counter. It will be eaten quickly, so there's no need to refrigerate it. When we go out to dinner, we always ask for extra butter when we sit down even if rolls aren't served!

Since our milk, cheese, and butter were so great and we worked so hard, Dad thought we ought to be making more money. Farmers had no negotiating power. He spent years trying to organize local farmers for the National Farmers Organization (NFO), a nonprofit organization that asked farmers to become members and agree to let NFO negotiate contracts for better pricing for their milk. Farmers took whatever big agricultural companies like Borden offered for their milk. This was an intolerable situation for Dad. He believed in collective bargaining. Organizing for the National Farmers Organization was a no-pay job, but he worked hard. He helped organize milk-dumping protests in the mid-1960s. Farmers emptied their milk cans into ditches rather than taking them to cheese factories. It was sad to see milk dumped in ditches, sad for the lost income for poor farm families, and sad for the waste of food. Some farmers went so far as to slaughter animals in front of the media. That backfired as people thought that slaughtering animals for purposes of publicity was outrageous. Dad didn't participate in that.

Dad put his heart into NFO advocacy, but it wasn't successful. He said, "Farmers are the last cowboys. They wouldn't organize even if it was important to their livelihood to do so. Farmers enjoy their independence too much."

He was sad to see his efforts to save family farms go unrewarded.

Dad taught me to get behind an effort, put my heart in it, and stick to it. He felt that doing the right thing was better than doing nothing, even if you lose. That's probably how I got into a campaign to abolish corporal punishment in Ohio schools during the mid-1980s. As a school psychologist, I was asked to be a witness to a paddling, something I had never seen. I was shocked. When I started this advocacy, over sixty thousand schoolchildren in Ohio's public schools were paddled annually. Many were paddled multiple times. Every public school in Ohio could use it, and school boards were not allowed to ban it based on an attorney general's opinion. Every education organization representing teachers, administrators, and school boards fought ban legislation except for a handful like the PTA and school psychologists. It was a long fight, over twenty years. We had twelve bills to ban its use introduced in the legislature during those years. We lost most of the time, but we always tried to get some restriction on its use into law rather than go away empty-handed. "Those paddling folks know how to play the game," said an Ohio School Boards Association lobbyist who opposed our efforts to ban school corporal punishment. We achieved incremental victories including a measure which permitted local districts to ban it, a measure requiring schools to submit annual reports to the State Board of Education on the number of kids paddled, and a measure requiring them to have community studies on discipline if they chose to keep paddling. Eventually, most school boards banned it voluntarily. It was too much bother to keep it, and they feared lawsuits for paddling injuries. They also had a little fear of us. We bestowed Top Hitter Awards of Dishonor on big paddling districts and courted media attention to their paddling numbers.

Our public education effort finally brought about a complete ban on public school corporal punishment by the Ohio legislature in 2009. Fifty organizations united with us in a coalition to end it, and Ohio joined twenty-nine other states that had already banned paddling. I memorialized the effort in the book *Breaking the Paddle: Ending School Corporal Punishment* (2013).

Because our efforts were successful, hundreds of thousands of schoolchildren in Ohio have not known the fear of and the pain from being hit with boards. No more "Grab your ankles and take your whacks!" in Ohio.

CHAPTER 12

Childhood Memories

When I was a child, my closest friend lived a mile away. I couldn't run over to share a secret or play a game, and I certainly couldn't text or Snapchat anyone. I was lucky to come from a big family where there were plenty of kids to provide companionship.

Ludwig Family (1954) Barbara, David, Nadine (back row), Sarah, Lynda, Lin, Franklin (front row)

Barbara, David, and I are close in age, but Lynda and Lin didn't come along until I was almost a teenager. Besides the disgust that overcame us when we realized our parents did *that*, my sister and I were not thrilled about babysitting. Having built-in help meant our parents shopped, worked outdoors, and enjoyed a busy social life whenever they wanted. It was fun having babies around at first, but it soon became tedious. I'd often mutter to myself that I never wanted to see another baby in my lifetime. However, my childcare skills were an advantage when I married and had children of my own. I had no anxieties about bringing a baby home from the hospital. I knew just what to do.

My two older siblings and I, who are closest in age, lived in a different world than the last two, Lynda and Lin. The oldest children grew up in the fifties, which were comfortable, hopeful, and secure. We were the tail end of the Silent Generation. Civil rights wasn't a big issue, or at least we didn't know about it. I knew nothing about the extent of racism. Feminism was latent. We didn't have problems with drugs. We didn't know they existed. We were prim and proper and were conformists. Mom and Dad were young and kept a tight hold on our behavior. The row of photos of the three older children on their bedroom dresser was not decorative. We had curfews in high school. Mom got up and turned over our photos when we came home from a night out. God help you if it wasn't down at curfew. It meant you didn't go out on dates for weeks. I didn't break that rule.

My younger siblings had only each other as playmates. Lynda invented imaginary friends she named Hymer and P. Reimer, who lived under the dining room table. She had tea and long chats with them. We still tease her about her invisible friends. At a family gathering in California, my brother Dave put a life-size doll he bought at a garage sale in a chair at the dining room table. Her place seating card said, "P. Reimer." Lynda laughed heartily. Dave sent P. Reimer to Lynda in Ohio after the visit. Lynda says, "I really don't have room for her, but I am keeping her to take her with me to the nursing home in case I am lonely."

By the time Lynda and Lin were teens in the mid-1960s, the culture was changing to one of disillusionment, anger, and protest. The Vietnam War became unpopular, and anti-war activists marched even in smaller towns. Grievances by African Americans were much more clamorous. Society had changed to youth with long hair, drugs, and anti-authority behavior. Kids called police "pigs." It seemed like a lawless time. Lin remembers teachers and students getting into physical fights. The murder of two students by another student shook our community when he was in high school.

My great-uncle John, Grandpa Ludwig's brother, drove up in his Nash Rambler for a visit to the farm one day when Lin and Lynda were in their teens. He lived in Oshkosh and was a successful entrepreneur. He owned box factories and car dealerships and was reputed to be the biggest stockholder in Wisconsin Power and Light. We were so excited for his visit—maybe he would shake a little fairy dust on our family. Instead, we found out that our devout Catholic great-uncle wanted Lin to become a priest and Lynda to become a nun. He told them he would take them to Rome if they would go into a seminary and nunnery. The sixties wasn't a great time to recruit kids for religious training. Lynda and Lin didn't bite.

Mom and Dad were tired, and the younger kids didn't experience the same kind of oversight the older children had. Mom said she couldn't keep track of Lynda because she would be out the door and "gone to who knows where." Lin joined the army to avenge the deaths of friends and neighbors. He was set to deploy with the 101st Airborne Division when Mom took matters into her own hands. She wrote Melvin Laird, the US Secretary of Defense and a former Wisconsin congressman, to ask for help in getting him back on the farm where they needed him. I don't know if he was the one who got my brother home, but it was consistent with Mom's strategies to go right to the top. Lin said he was lucky not to be part of over twenty thousand troops in that division injured or killed in Vietnam.

Being in a large family meant in-house friends as well as kids with whom to fight. Fighting in our family wasn't physical; it usually meant name-calling or protestations about others not doing their fair share of work. "You didn't do your share of work! You took more than your share of cookies!" Fairness was an important concept in our house. The girls were sure the boys were treated like princelings because they didn't have to help in the house. When the boys were too young to work in the barn, the girls were already required to do housework, gardening, and working in the fields. Mom's excuse for exempting boys from housework was that boys shouldn't have to help in the house. There were no substitute jobs. Being a boy gave them superior status. But we got even. When Mom and Dad were gone, the authority figures were the older sisters. "Pick up the broom, only boy. Get to work!" My taunts were another notation made in Mom's catalog of my shenanigans.

David said he doesn't mind the way we treated him. "My sisters taught me to live with strong women," he said.

Role expectations for men and women at that time reinforced my parents' treatment of us. Boys could expect to inherit a farm or get help buying one. It followed the German tradition of keeping the family nearby and giving males a start in life. My brothers went off to college with a small steady income from cattle they owned, and Lin even had a car with an 8-track cassette, a big deal then. Girls were expected to marry well and were therefore not given much support. Dad gave me the name of the richest farmer in the county who had a son my age, so I knew my supposed target. There was no discussion of college for me. Mom wanted me to go to Milwaukee after high school to become a secretary for the Pfister Hotel. The hotel opened in 1893 and was then, as it is now, a Grande Dame Milwaukee hotel. I think Mom's encouragement to head to Milwaukee stemmed from her suppressed desire.

Sibling tiffs usually ended soon after they started because we depended on one another. Working as a team was imperative to our humming farm business and everyone's safety. We rarely carried grudges, and each of us decided that no disagreement with a family member was worth a long-term estrangement. It's a practice that continues today. Since we're divided on politics, it takes work to maintain our good relationships. But because we observed Mom's lifetime score-counting, estrangements, and grudges, we decided we were not going to do the same.

Our kitchen table was the main work space in the house. Dad did his township treasurer job, the kids did homework, Mom sewed and canned, and our family ate together. Mom cooked breakfast and two big meals a day. The largest was dinner, which she served at noon. Farmers needed a hardy midday meal to keep them going. Even when she went to an assisted living facility in her one-hundredth year, Mom used the farm term *dinner* for lunch.

We rented freezer space at Hauser's grocery store in Stetsonville for the slaughter meat from our farm. Mom used it to create heaping plates of stews, New England boiled dinner (pork or beef slow cooked with carrots, cabbage, and potatoes), fried chicken, pork with a side of sauerkraut (renamed *liberty cabbage* during WWII due to anti-German feelings), mashed or baked potatoes, and canned vegetables. Mom could take a jar of our home-canned beef from the basement and turn it into a tasty dinner.

I don't recall eating steak when I was young, although sometimes we ate game food like venison, which was tough and had a wild taste. It was inedible to me for reasons beyond the flavor. Dad seldom hunted, and his last time came after he saw our response to a deer hanging from a tree in the backyard. We kids stood at the window pointing to the dead animal that looked like Bambi. We refused to eat a murdered Disney character.

There wasn't much fresh fish, but when Grandpa Milles fished in the summer, he'd bring home his catch. Every month, he'd also treat us to smoked fish that he'd buy with his "welfare check" (that's what Dad called Social Security payments). Once we picked out the fat and bones, we enjoyed the smoked fish. Barbara remembers a door-to-door salesman who sold frozen cod in ice blocks that she recalls being delicious. And Grandpa Ludwig brought fish from his ice-fishing expeditions on occasion.

There was no pizza delivery, Chinese takeout, or McDonald's drive-throughs. Eating out meant dining at the house of a relative or a stop at the A&W or Milly's Bowling Alley for a hamburger.

Mom enjoyed baking, so we usually had pies, rolls, and cakes with boiled frosting. Today when I go to the supermarket, I'll sometimes buy a doughnut because they make me think of Mom's confections. I'm always so disappointed. They never compare to the magic Mom created. I can still remember the pungent smell of yeast dough she'd roll out and cut into rounds. One by one, she'd drop them into steaming hot lard where they'd turn golden brown. She would lift them from the fat with a large slotted spoon and roll them in sugar. Small waiting hands grabbed them feverishly. The doughnuts never got cold, and none were ever left for the next day's breakfast. They were gone before the lard in the fry pan congealed. We loved the feeling of the sugary crust on our tongues. Everything Mom baked was delicious, but to me, nothing surpassed her sugary, warm yeast doughnuts.

Between school and chores, we didn't have much time to get into trouble. But when we did, it meant another work assignment added to the list of jobs we already had. We might be sent to knock potato plant bugs into jars with a few drops of gasoline at the bottom (organic pest control, 1950s style), weed the garden, or pull wild mustard from the field. Picking up rocks from the field was a regular chore, but it was also given as punishment.

"We get a bigger crop of rocks each year," we grumbled as we threw rocks on the trailer behind the tractor. Freezing and thawing in winter pushed new rocks up. They could ruin farm equipment and had to be removed. It was backbreaking work. They were dirty and heavy, and we didn't wear gloves. We used the stones to fill a dry streambed in the back, forty acres. "Harvesting" rocks was one of our worst jobs.

Sometimes we were sent to sprout potatoes in the dank, dark basement so they remained edible over the winter or go into the henhouse to collect eggs. I hated both jobs, but I hated the henhouse job more. We had to reach into the nests and extract warm, dirty eggs that we'd clean and box. The chickens didn't like it any more than we did. They squawked as they flew at us. We got out as fast as we could.

Picking tiny wild raspberries no bigger than a fingertip was another punishment. It was a dreadful job. The thorny raspberry bushes were in the woods a quarter of a mile from our house, and it took hours to fill a quart syrup can. Mosquitos swarmed, and the thorns attacked as we sweated under the hot sun collecting berries. We'd grouse about how evil and mean our parents were. "Let's pack peanut butter sandwiches and run away into the woods," we strategized. Barbara mused, "Remember Grandma Anna said some Indians lived in this forest when she was little. They used to steal apple pies cooling on the windowsills." "No more Indians to worry about, but remember the black bears Daddy told us about?" I said. We quickly discarded the woods-runaway idea and decided we would have to tough it out with our mean parents.

It wasn't a regular punishment, but sometimes our parents spanked us. It was usually done with a hand, but willow tree branches or a hairbrush were sometimes used. I resent it to this day. It usually happened because we were misunderstood or my parents hadn't listened to or tried to find out what preceded the supposed misbehavior. Mom believed that spanking worked. She said we obeyed because we feared a spanking. I explained that it might have stopped us from doing what they didn't want for the moment, but it made us resentful and careful enough not to do it when they were there. I told Mom, "You just taught us to be sneaky." If we were going to get into mischief, we would have a lookout warn us if they were near.

Mom spanked us more often than Dad. Dad once spanked me when I was six for telling what he believed was a lie. I'd told our neighbors that Barbara and I were going to sing on the radio program, the Morris B. Sachs Amateur Hour. What Mom and Dad didn't put together was that before I shared the exciting news with neighbors, I'd asked them if we could perform on the radio show, and they'd said yes. They probably were busy and not listening. It was miscommunication between a child and parent that resulted in corporal punishment. When I tried to explain that I hadn't lied, they didn't listen. They didn't care to hear explanations or excuses. It was hard to fight the adult system. We were powerless against them. Mom added the "lie" to her growing list of my mischievous acts.

When I was older, I coedited and published a book of children's art and writing entitled *This Hurts Me More than It Hurts You: In Words and Pictures, Children Share How Spanking Hurts and What to Do Instead*. It's used in parenting programs to teach parents the effects of corporal punishment as felt by children.

I sent a copy to Mom, but not even that convinced her. She died unrepentant about spanking. When she was in her nineties, she said she couldn't have raised five children without spanking. She followed that by saying, "Besides, I helped give you a cause and some fame."

Seeds of perfectionism were sown in us by both parents, but Mom led the charge. She was adept at finding room for improvement. "Take a look at the floor. It's still not clean. Get the broom" or "Who made this bed? The sheet is showing below the blanket hem" or "There is still spilled grain on the granary floor. Go get a broom." We usually performed our chores well for our ages, but we pushed ourselves to improve. I still criticize my work and think I could have done better. It seldom meets the vision I have for it, and I passed this on to my sons. I often checked their homework and asked them to go over it to see if it could be improved.

"Are you happy with that?" I would ask them and give a couple of suggestions for improvement. It's no wonder that my grown children sometimes refer to me as The Drill. I was a pretty good drill sergeant and had professional training from my mother.

As kids, we didn't often feel mistreated. We understood the value of money and didn't ask for expensive things. We knew that we lived as well as most people we knew. Maybe better. Overall, childhood was a fun, happy time.

Growing up on the farm taught us a lot about time management, medicine, caring for animals, and finances. We had a better sense of handling money as kids than some adults do today. We spent a lot of time with our parents, and we had daily exposure to their values and knowledge. We learned not only what they believed, but they showed us how their beliefs fit into our daily lives. I often remembered Dad's gentle prodding to get me to know the richest farmer's son, his idea of my future husband. That was not a value I shared. It wasn't in my plan. I wasn't going to be a farmer's wife. No matter how comfortable and secure it was living on the farm, I never forgot that I wanted to leave as soon as I could.

CHAPTER 13

A Little Fun

We didn't have much fun after school because we always had housework or farm chores, but summertime was different. Even though planting, weeding, harvesting crops, gardening, and canning food filled out days, there was still time to play. Our inventory of toys was sparse, but we made do with a scooter, a couple of bicycles, a doll buggy, some balls and bats, and metal dollhouses. The tiny metal dwellings were home to our paper dolls, and we made the furniture, rugs, drapes, and wall coverings.

The younger children had a horse, Pixie, and sometimes the older children rode it, although everyone who did usually ended up on the ground. "We should have named him Crazy Horse," Lin remembers. Barbara said, "I think he deliberately ran under the apple tree so the branches would knock me off." Pixie was the offspring of a mustang who was sent to be butchered by a mink farmer to feed his mink. The mustang eyed the mink farmer's prize quarter horse across a fence. He jumped the fence and left the prize horse impregnated with Pixie, who turned out to be as crazy as the doomed mustang. The Amish couldn't break it, and gelding did not change his behavior. I was too smart to ride and get knocked off that dumb horse.

Empty tin cans became pretend telephones when we attached a taut wire between them. We swore they worked, but it was probably just the vibrations of speech that we felt. Blankets tossed over clotheslines became tents. It was an exciting adventure until it got dark or we heard scary noises. Dad made a wooden playhouse that we adored until we found a long black snake in it. We quickly ran out screaming and abandoned it.

We played Annie-Annie Over, a game that required players to throw a small old red rubber ball over the roof and run around the house trying to avoid being tagged by whoever retrieved the ball. Once you were tagged, you had to join that team and chase your old team members. Cornfields next to the house made wonderful venues for hide-and-seek. Dad said corn was usually knee-high by the Fourth of July, which meant easy hiding through most of the summer. The games were even merrier when cousins or neighbor children joined us.

Rubbernecking or listening in on the shared telephone party line was also a favorite pastime. We could hear what neighbors were discussing. It was a sneaky way of finding out if a neighbor was sick, if someone had polio, or if a big argument was underway. Sometimes we enjoyed someone else's misfortunes. Mom liked to rubberneck too, but since she and her sister spoke Lithuanian, rubberneckers couldn't pass on their chatter. When we were teenagers, Barbara and I used to pretend we were the other person when boys called. I don't think they caught on, and we laughed a lot about that.

In the summer, Dad sometimes drove us to Sackett Lake. We didn't go often because it was thirty miles away, and when we did go, we never stayed long. Farm chores took precedence. Mom didn't swim, and if we walked into the water above our belly buttons, she'd flap her arms and yell for us to return to the shallow part. "Franklin! Franklin! Make them come back!" she yelled. Dad liked to throw us up in the air and let us plop into the cool water. That terrified me. I'd already absorbed Mom's fear. None of us learned to swim well. There was no public swimming pool nearby or one in the high school for the older children. The younger kids fared better since their high school had a swimming pool. I am a dog-paddler swimmer and am the first person to put on a life vest when boating.

Summertime also meant making root beer. Coca-Cola and Pepsi were around, but our parents didn't buy it. We often asked to stop at a Medford drive-in to get A&W root beer. It was delicious on a hot day, served in big frosty mugs. Our parents usually denied our requests. "We'll have some of our root beer. It's better than A&W," Dad said to soothe our disappointment. He wasn't wrong. Our root beer, especially with a little homemade ice cream, was divine.

We made root beer with ingredients like ginger, vanilla, cinnamon, and sassafras to which we added cane sugar and heated the mixture. Molasses and yeast (for carbonation) were added; and it was left to cool and ferment for a few minutes, then funneled into bottles, and sealed quickly with caps. We stored them in the basement. Sometimes we would hear "Bang! Bang! Bang!" from the basement. Bottle caps blew off, causing a huge bang. The metal caps ricocheted around the basement. Foaming root beer ran all over the floor. Obviously, our carbonation plan didn't work. We probably measured the yeast wrong, which was disappointing because we failed to do something correctly, and we'd have fewer bottles of precious root beer.

We made our own ice cream too. It started with Mom's special custard pudding of cream, egg yolks, and sugar. It was put in a two-quart metal container that sat inside a wooden bucket full of crushed ice and salt. The salt keeps the ice from freezing before the ice cream is hard. Each of us kids would take turns cranking the handle that turned the container in its ice bath. It was hard work, and it took a long time. It wore out our arms, but the ice cream—

whether it was chocolate, vanilla, or some other flavor—was wonderful.

Summer Friday nights meant outdoor movies in Dorchester, a little town five miles away. Mom and Dad would bring a blanket for us to sit on while they went shopping in the grocery store or stood around gossiping with other farmers. The movies were mostly westerns with Roy Rogers and Gene Autry. The screen was blurry, and the sound was either too loud or scarcely audible; but we loved it. Dad bought us cylindrical malted milk ice cream treats called Cho Chos that were on a stick and wrapped in paper. We warmed up the paper with our hands to make removing it easy. Yum! We treasured every lick. Life was good!

Another summertime activity was catching lightning bugs on the front lawn. We'd sit in the grass in the dark and catch the fairylike creatures in quart jars and watch them flash. How could these tiny creatures make such a bright light? We figured it was males showing off for females. How wonderful it would have been to Google "lightning bugs" and find answers to our questions. We would have learned that they were beetles, not flies or bugs, and that we were right about males trying to attract females. What we didn't know is that females would signal back and sometimes eat their suitors. Having such interesting scientific information would have been entertaining and made us more interested in science.

Our family loved music. We took piano lessons from our cousin Franklin Fritsche, the local postmaster. We liked singing, and most of us kids played in the high school band or sang in the choir. The music we listened to that set our toes tapping was polka music with titles like "Beer Barrel Polka," "Tick Tock Polka," "She's Too Fat for Me Polka," "In Heaven There Is No Beer—That's Why We Drink It Here Polka," and "Pennsylvania Polka." We heard polka music on the radio and at weddings. Polka bands usually had an accordion or two, drums, banjo or guitar, piano, and maybe a saxophone and bass. Sometimes there was a vocalist. It was great fun to drive in our car in the 1940s and 1950s and have a family sing-along with Dad. Mom never joined in. We sang World War II—era songs like "Lili Marlene" and "Boogie Woogie Bugle Boys" and hummed along to "Take the A Train." Dad knew the words to every popular song during those years. Here's a silly one we liked to sing:

She's Too Fat for Me Polka

Here's a silly jingle,
You can sing it night or noon
Here's the words, that's all you need
'Cause I just sang the tune:

Oh, I don't want her, you can have her
She's too fat for me
She's too fat for me
She's too fat for me
I don't want her, you can have her,
She's too fat for me
She's too fat
She's too fat
She's too fat for me.

We loved to dance to lively polkas, flying around the room to this fast 2/4 beat folk music. Now when we play polka music at family gatherings, my brother David invites my sisters and me to dance. We dance like teens, or at least we feel like teens for a song or two. By then, we are out of breath. At Mom's one-hundredth birthday party, she danced with David. It wasn't sprightly, but she lifted her feet to the music of the accordionist. When I'm in my home office, I love to turn on Pandora and blast polka music out of my Sonos speakers while I dance around the room. My husband peeks in, scratches his head, and quickly shuts the door. I'm certain he's afraid that the neighbors will find out his wife is a madwoman.

The onset of winter meant a whole new world of activities and fun. All the frigid precipitation turned our farm into a winter wonderland where snow forts and snowmen were built and snowball battles ensued. Country roads had snowbanks eight to ten feet high. From the car window, the road was a forbidding bluish-white ice tunnel. Snow was piled layer upon layer for up to six months, and some Wisconsin days were thirty degrees below zero. A frozen creek on the farm of Herb and Edna Voit, Dad's sister and her husband, was our ice-skating rink.

Barbara and I would strap on skates and glide for a mile or so through pasturelands and woods. There were no Zambonis to clear a path for us, so sometimes we had to walk through or jump over snowbanks on the creek. We pictured ourselves as Sonja Henie, the beautiful Norwegian figure skater who starred in movies we had seen. Our noses were as red as Rudolph's, and even heavy mittens couldn't keep our hands warm; but it didn't stop us from skating for hours to our internal Sonja Henie-music soundtrack with our scarves fluttering behind us.

We had wooden skis that would make our grandchildren laugh. "How can you even ski down a bunny slope on those?" They'd laugh. Not only did we not have carbon fiber and laminated wood skis, but our skis were just thin sculpted pine boards. We vigorously waxed the bottom of our skis before we used them. They had metal bindings and leather straps. The straps didn't hold our feet in tight, and we didn't use poles; so there were a lot of falls. We lacked fashionable ski jackets, flex ski boots, and waterproof leggings. I should also mention that we weren't gliding down a picturesque mountain swooshing past alpines. Dad drove a car or tractor with ropes tied to the back that we'd hang onto as he pulled us on the roads or through the fields on mounds of snow. It was a little dicey when we left the snowbanks along the roads to cross driveways or ditches as more falls occurred. I'm confident the rustic skiing was as fun for us as it is for my grandchildren who ski on lovely trails of Aspen, Breckinridge, or Telluride. It was the only world we knew.

Dad was always our cheerful Wisconsin weather apologist. Wisconsin winter weather needs apologies. I remember calling him after I had moved away to ask about the weather. He'd say, "It's twenty below zero, but the sun is bright and warm. It feels good." In Northern Wisconsin, snow and ice never melt in the winter, and the cold rivals that of the arctic tundra. Dad used tire chains and sand to provide traction in snowdrifts and icy ruts. We weighted the car trunk with bags of sand. Today, I'm seldom where there is snow. I head as far south as I need to go to escape the winter "wonderland." I like images of winter, but I hate being in snow and cold. It was one more reason I wanted to escape from Wisconsin.

When snowstorms hit, we shoveled what seemed like a mile-long driveway with snow up to three feet high. It took hours to clear. As a thank you, Dad would take us to a movie at the Avon Theater in Medford. It opened in the year I was born. What a wonderful treat! Its interior was glorious. It mimicked a canal in Venice that transported us away from our small rural community. I put my hands together and prayed, "Please, God, I want see Venice some day!"

Kids who caused problems got kicked out and had their dime admission returned, so we were always on our best behavior. We didn't risk being noisy and silly. We sat in our seats delighted by cartoons like *Woody Woodpecker*, *Tom and Jerry*, and *Mickey Mouse* and westerns like *Red River* and *The Treasure of Sierra Madre* that flickered on the screen. Between the feature and the cartoon, newsreels of WWII mesmerized us. It was through the action shots of soldiers that the war became real.

We also had the radio. It was not only a source of information, but it also entertained us. When I helped Dad with the tax rolls, we listened to the University of Wisconsin basketball games. Bud Foster coached the Badgers during my youth and had winning seasons until the 1960s. We also listened to comedy programs like *Fibber McGee and Molly*, *Jack Benny*, *Ozzie and Harriet*, and *The Life of Riley*. We envied kids whose parents let them send in box tops to get secret decoder badges and rings from adventure programs like *Sky King* and *Captain Midnight*.

When we were a little older, we tuned in to soap operas like *The Guiding Light* and *Ma Perkins*. I can still hear the introduction to *Our Gal Sunday*: "Can this girl from a little mining town in the west find happiness as the wife of a rich and titled Englishman?"

Maybe she did, maybe she didn't. That part I don't remember.

Dad's favorite treat was popcorn with homemade fudge drizzled on it. He'd make it for us to snack on when we listened to the radio. He also made crunchy sea foam candy that he cooked to a perfect consistency without a candy thermometer. With five children, there were no left-overs. Our family could devour a half gallon of ice cream at one sitting. Spumoni was our favorite.

We got a TV when I was in high school, but the only semiviewable station was out of Green Bay. We'd gather around the big boxy piece of furniture with a fourteen-inch screen, squinting our eyes to try to make out what was hap-pening. Black-and-white figures were blurry and swathed in snowflakes; it was still exciting. We all tried to be the first to interpret what we were seeing.

Somewhere between fun and work was the 4-H club that my siblings and I belonged to. The *H*s stood for Head, Health, Hands, and Hearts. We learned about gardening, food, nutrition, raising animals, woodworking, public speaking, and photography. Small groups of farm kids that ranged in age from ten to seventeen met regularly with an adult leader. I can still remember the pledge recited at each meeting:

I pledge my Head to clearer thinking,
my Heart to greater loyalty,
my Hands to larger service,
and my Health to better living,
for my club, my community,
my country, and my world.

We learned to sew and cook at home, but 4-H helped us share and learn how to judge and improve our skills. Barbara and I gave demonstrations on how to make yeast rolls and how to make an apron. When I was doing substitute teaching in the early 1970s, I reported to a middle school home economics class in Worthington, Ohio, where the lesson plan called for teaching how to set in a sleeve in a garment. Most subs probably would have brought out a film or handed out some written busy work. I demonstrated the process. 4-H had taught me how to do that.

I was thirteen or fourteen when I won a 4-H trip to be a judge in food and nutrition at the state fair in West Allis, a suburb of Milwaukee. It was my first independent excursion away from home. I stayed in a rudimentary building on the fairgrounds with other 4-H kids. There was so much to see and do, but we didn't have much freedom to walk around. I was able to peek through slats between the wallboard where we stayed to watch the fairgoers. I saw a diverse population that I'd only seen in newspapers and magazines like *Look*, *Life*, and *Time*. I met other farm kids involved in 4-H, but it was the people whose faces didn't look like mine that fascinated me. I wanted to know what they knew, what was important to them, where they lived, and why they behaved as they did. I couldn't wait to be in a bigger world than what I grew up in.

Mom was shy and determined that we should not carry that burden. She encouraged us to join the 4-H public speaking program and often helped us with speech ideas. In the eighth grade, I won a countywide speaking contest and gave my speech about conservation on WIGM radio in Medford. Another 4-H kid and I sat at a table at the radio station and read our winning speeches.

"4-H offered me a great experience as a nerdy little farm boy," says brother Dave. He remembers winning a state 4-H speaking contest. He earned a trip to Chicago sponsored by WGN Radio. At age twelve, Dad dropped him off at the train station in Wausau. He was met at the train station in Chicago. "Along with some other Midwest states' winners, we were introduced on WGN radio. That evening, we were taken to a stage play, *No Time for Sergeants*."

Our 4-H club was under the Taylor County Extension Program, which brought science education, and modern agricultural practices to rural communities. Claire Abrahamson, a county extension director, became a mentor to me and many other kids. When I was in elementary school, I sang "When You Come to the End of a Perfect Day" at the Medford Avon Theater at her urging. I stood in front of what felt like a vast audience but was closer to twenty-five people (mostly relatives) and belted out the lyrics with my small, reedy voice as a pianist played along. Having someone interested in me was elating, and that experience was shared by other Taylor County kids through 4-H.

Mrs. Abrahamson had a photographer take my photo which she sent to Hollywood producers who were seeking a pretty farm girl for an upcoming movie. Mom styled my blond hair like a Swiss Miss with braids wrapped around the top of my head. After we mailed the photo, I was eager for the postman to deliver something from sunny California. Maybe I would be a movie star! As the days passed and no golden envelope arrived, I gave up my acting career.

Nadine: Farm Girl Photo

Mrs. Abrahamson made me feel important, made me believe in myself, and made me aim high. Because of her, naysayers never deter me. She made me aware of the value in adults noticing and recognizing children, which is one of the reasons I happily became a founding board member of Support for Talented Students in 1983. The Ohio non-profit provides funds for gifted, underprivileged students to participate in music, art, science, acting, and writing in programs outside school hours. Support for Talented Students has given hundreds of central Ohio students scholarships and is still in business serving kids today. Mrs. Abrahamson helped me believe I would someday be able to go to college and see a bigger world.

CHAPTER 14

Work! Work! No Child Labor Laws for Farm Kids

Almost three-fourths of US child labor was in agriculture when I was a child. Since 1938, children laboring in factories are protected, but those laws don't protect farm kids. The work hours for children in my family were long and hard. My sister Lynda says that shoveling grain was the worst. "It was hot, sticky, and a huge pain in the ass." As a kid, she thought inhaling the grain dust would kill her. Of course, our parents felt that we were living a soft life—easy and carefree—compared to their childhood.

School ended in May, just in time for children to help with spring planting. Hay, corn, and oats were crops for cattle on our farm. Once the planting was complete, we helped feed, milk, and clean up after cows. Sometimes we turned work into fun. We'd pretend we were cowboys rounding up the steers during cattle drives down dirt roads. We'd take the young stock a mile from our farm to their summer home. It was twenty acres of uncultivated land with a wood that sheltered heifers from heat and a spring that provided water. By winter, we had a barn full of cows to feed. We had black-and-white Holstein cows and brown-and-white Guernseys. Holsteins gave more milk than Guernseys. Guernsey cows are more docile than Holsteins and give creamy milk with high butterfat content. We used their milk to make ice cream and butter. Farmers get paid for their milk with formulas using weight and butterfat content. My favorite, Rosie, was among the Guernsey cows.

Cows on our farm were artificially inseminated, but the birth process was natural. Cows' pregnancies are about nine months long, and Dad generally knew when they were close to giving birth. Cows lie down to push the calf out, but if Dad didn't see the front feet and head come out first, he'd reach inside the mother to turn the calf or pull it out. After the calf is born, the mother cow licks off the blood and afterbirth tissue. Then she gives the newborn a nudge with her nose to encourage it to stand. I didn't much like watching the messy birth process, but I loved watching the little calves take their first steps to their mother's udder. Calves bleated for their mothers, and the cows answered them with longing moos. We trained the calves to drink out of pails so the mother's milk could be sold. The calves were sold a few weeks after they were born for veal. We kept a few though, like Rosie.

Franklin and the Milking Machine

Our cows spent the warm days of spring, summer, and fall eating grass in pastures. We kids would go to the grazing fields to round them up and take them to the barn for milking. This happened every morning and evening like clockwork. The cows were always eager to go to the barn. Maybe it was because their udders were bursting with milk or because they knew they'd get fed. During the summer and fall, our job was to get the cows' food into the barn, granary, and silo. Their menu consisted of ground-up oats, bones, and corncobs sprinkled with mineral and vitamin supplements. They gobbled it up like it was a blue-ribbon dessert. During the winter, they stayed in their stanchions, and hay was their primary food source.

Cows loved to eat clover in the field and harvested as hay. Sweet-smelling clover fields mixed with timothy, rye, and fescue grasses turned into hay around the Fourth of July and were ready to harvest. Dad, like all farmers, gauged the weather and always kept a wary eye on the sky. Dad had to predict when there would be three to four days of dry sunny weather so the cut grass could dry. If it was wet when we harvested it, it would mold, and cows would turn their noses up at it. Inedible hay became cow bedding. Farming is a risky business since the weather is not under a farmer's control.

"Don't go into a business where God is your partner," Dad advised his grandchildren.

A mower drawn by a tractor cut the hay. Sometimes the blades hit small animals hiding in the tall grass. I once looked back while I was mowing and saw a bloody mess of dead baby rabbits. I grimaced, turned my head, and kept going. I didn't want a close look.

After cutting the hay, we raked it into rows with a farm tool with metal teeth that was dragged by the tractor. In our parents' day and early in our lives, loose dry hay was loaded by a hay loader into wagons and taken to the hay-mow in the barn. The haymow, which is the second story of a barn, stored our hay. When Mom and Dad were first married, horses pulled a rope that lifted a hay fork from a hay-filled wagon and guided it up a track to the haymow. When the large fork hit a switch, it dropped a load of loose hay in the haymow. Later, a tractor pulled the wagons and ran the pulley for the hay fork. We often had to go up into the hot dusty second story of the barn to spread the hay, so it didn't bunch up under the track. We went through a lot of "bug juice" (that's what we called the Kool-Aid) on those hot sweaty days.

By the time I was in high school, a tractor-drawn baler machine rolled up hay bales for cow food. Often it was one of us kids driving the machines. I learned to drive a tractor when I was eight or nine years old. I couldn't reach the brakes, but I could reach the key. Dad taught me how to turn off the motor to stop the tractor.

My sons often helped on the farm in summers. It didn't take them long to discover how hard it was to stack the skin-scratching bales onto wagons. The bales were round or rectangular, heavy to lift, and difficult to stack. Wagons loaded wrong would tip over, so you always had to pay close attention.

In spring, rows of corn were planted in a prepared field with churned soil free from weeds and rocks. Farm equipment pulled by a tractor would cultivate the soil until the crop had a head start on the weeds. Herbicides became popular around 1950, but their harmful effects were unknown.

Franklin, Lynda and Lin Checking the Corn Crop

When fall rolled around and the corn was ripe, cornstalks were cut and bundled into shocks. The shocks stood upright, like a cornstalk tepee, so air could circulate to keep it from rotting. It was hot work, with bugs and spiders, scratchy hay, and heavy bundles. After they dried, we'd toss the shocks in a wagon and transport them to the chopper next to the barn and silo. The dried corn and stalks went into a machine that chopped it and blew it into the forty-foot-high silo. After fermentation, the chopped corn became *silage*, cow food.

Later, we had a corn harvester that cut and chopped the standing cornstalks in the field. It blew the chopped corn into a four-sided wagon. Dave remembers that the front wall of the wagon operated off the tractor's power takeoff to move the chopped corn backward onto a conveyor and into the silo filler. Lin remembers, "If the fields were wet and muddy, we often chained two or even three tractors together to pull the heavy equipment and wagons. The head tractor's front wheels would come off the ground like a rearing horse. This was very dangerous. You could flip over and be trapped under it. A neighbor died like that."

We shucked leftover corn. We sat on the floor of an outbuilding pulling leaves off big stacks of corncobs. As we shucked, we threw the cobs into a pile to dry out so they could be taken to the feed mill to grind for cattle food.

Oats were planted in May. It was a month or so before the plants grew large enough to fend for themselves against weeds, so we pulled them by hand. Lynda hated it. Now when she drives past fields of yellow mustard weed, she finds herself wondering why people aren't out in the field pulling the weeds. "That was the job I hated the most. Acres and acres of yellow mustard seemed to grow before my eyes. Farm kids today are darn lucky for having pesticides!" she remarked.

As the oat field matured in late summer, soft winds turned it into an undulating dark-gold sea that went as far as a kid could see. We cut the oats with a binder pulled by a tractor. Once cut and tied into a bundle by the binder, the oats were dumped on the ground. The child labor crew put bundles into shocks to keep them dry and off the ground.

One of the summer's biggest events was when the threshing machine came. The thundering racket of a big steam engine twenty feet long and twelve feet high was loud enough to signal its arrival. In case you missed its clamorous arrival, the driver announced the thresher with a shrill whistle as he turned into the driveway. Neighboring farmers followed behind the thunderous engine with their tractors and wagons ready to tackle our oat fields. When they finished, they moved to a new farm to fill wagons with bundles that they'd feed into the clanging machine. Dust swirled as the grain and the straw separated. Straw became animal bedding in the winter, and the separated oats were bagged and taken to the feed mill where they were ground into cattle food.

Mom would bake for days before the thresher crew arrived, mostly dinner rolls and pies. She wanted to have the best food and the most heavily laden table in the neighborhood. Every meal was a contest, and the neighbor ladies were her competition. She grinned shyly when complimented by the men. Her helpers (us children) basked in her pride. She loved to recount a story about one of our neighbors who found her food superior. He complained that the stew they had at the previous house might have been a sick cow they saw in the yard a few days earlier. Mom loved that comment and treasured it up until her death. Some workers took a little beer and a brief rest before moving on to the next farm. Most of the men drank Kool-Aid or unpasteurized milk. This exciting summer event disappeared when farmers began buying combines—first, in partnership with others, and later, individually.

Farming is a physical job with danger lurking all around. According to a Wisconsin Farm-Related Fatality Report, 124 farm fatalities took place in 1950. The causes of most fatalities were firearms, drowning, animals, electrocution, and falling. But farm machinery accounted for the highest single cause. Tractors were the most dangerous, but cutting machinery, large augers, choppers, balers, combines, and big conveyor belts could cause the loss of fingers, hands, and arms. Silo fillers were also dangerous. The machine had a large gaping hole where farmers threw corn shocks in to be chopped by large blades and sent up a pipe to the silo. The filler sometimes got blocked, and farmers who were in a hurry wouldn't shut it off before removing the blockage. One of our neighbors fell into his silo filler while dislodging a blockage. The following winter when the family fed corn silage to the cows, they found some of his teeth and small body bones.

Wagons loaded poorly would turn over. Big animals were often the source of injuries. There were plenty of self-inflicted firearm injuries due to careless use of rifles during deer hunting season in the fall. Without a bright red or orange shirt or vest, you could be mistaken for an animal and shot by a member of a hunting party. My brother Dave recalls with anxiety that he almost shot his friend during a partridge hunting trip when they were fifteen. He forgot that he'd left the shotgun cocked and just missed his friend when it accidentally went off. He said he wouldn't have known what to do since emergency services were not readily available. Of course, he didn't have a smartphone to call for help. God help you if you were injured. Dirt roads were the only way to get to the nearest hospital that was ten miles away.

Dad got bruised by a cow and, at another time, fell out of the haymow, but I don't recall any significant injuries in our family, which is no real surprise. The same mother who kept us from venturing beyond our belly buttons at the swimming hole also made sure her family didn't get hurt.

My first husband, Jared Block, and I gave our three boys more freedom than many children had at their age. Our childhoods influenced our attitudes toward freedom. Jared told stories of running free and getting into fights and other mischief in Janesville, Wisconsin. He said his parents didn't keep much watch over him. Mom and Dad left us to plan our games and entertainment, and they let us drive cars and handle farm equipment at ages that might not be accepted as safe today.

When our three sons—Steve, Jeff, and Greg—were teenagers, we left them in Paris with Eurail Passes and a credit card. Leaving them with a cellphone and a SIM card wasn't an option. They didn't exist. "Don't worry, we'll be fine," they assured us. We told them to meet us in Athens, Greece, in two weeks when we would return from a Mediterranean cruise. I remember sitting in our Parisian hotel, trying to get a trip plan out of them. "Why don't you guys head for Lyon for your first stop?" I cajoled. I had maps strewn across the bed with my hand-drawn arrows pointing to interesting places to visit and where they might go in case of an emergency. They quietly resisted my planning efforts.

Apparently, they handled their freedom successfully as they showed up at 10:00 p.m. on the appointed day at our Hilton Hotel in Athens. But it wasn't until many years later that I heard about their adventures. My sons disregarded my idea that they begin their European journey in Lyon. After leaving Paris, they headed straight to the topless beaches of Nice. I shouldn't have been surprised that our creative boys had plans for their trip.

When my sons were teens, they baled hay, stacked hay wagons, drove tractors, helped Gramps in the barn, and took the place of hired help on the farm in the summer. They felt they were doing something that helped their grandparents, and in return for their hard work, Mom and Dad paid them. Visiting their grandparents meant a lot of freedom. They let the boys drive the car without a license and took them to the bar for Friday night fish fry dinners where they'd sometimes have a few sips of beer. They tried to find my dad's shotgun and cigarettes, but to no avail.

Initially, I worried about them but remembered that their grandma was a hawk about nosing out danger and keeping children safe. No one ever got hurt.

Picking strawberries was a backbreaking job that had us stooped over in the garden for hours. We'd fill multiple quart boxes that Mom would often give away to random visitors. We resented her generosity because we worked so hard to gather them. We thought they should remain with the family.

My childhood gardening experiences leave me feeling conflicted. As much as I like to watch plants grow, I'm not a gardener. I know the work it takes to till the soil and disk it to break up and pulverize the earth to prepare it for planting seeds or small plants. Then you need to fertilize, water, and weed. The only fun part to me is eating the produce. And if I'm being honest, grocery store strawberries taste as good as those in our garden. Today, I sometimes bring home pots of herbs like basil and thyme, and I grow house plants like ivy and succulents because they help make our air healthy and they're beautiful. My second husband, William Brown, planted a small orchard of fruit trees at our Florida house. That's as close to growing things as I need or want to be.

CHAPTER 15

A Self-Sufficient Farm

"I only spent fifty-three dollars in grocery stores for the whole year of 1937," Dad told me. Except for coffee, tea, flour, sugar, salt, pepper, baking soda, and spices, our farm kept us self-sufficient food-wise. Our basement was lined with shelves of canned vegetables, fruit, meat, and stoneware crocks of sauerkraut—a staple in German homes. We made sauerkraut from chopped cabbage that we'd put in crocks with layers of noniodized salt. Weighted plates were placed on top of the jars, then covered with a heavy board to keep the contents clean until the kraut was ready to can. The jars of the cut cabbage mixture were stored in our cool basement for four to six weeks. As the cabbage fermented, it produced a salty brine. I remember the acrid, sour smell of fermenting cabbage; surprisingly, I like the smell of sauerkraut. A bratwurst with fresh sauerkraut is delicious!

We had a garden about a quarter acre in size. It seemed much larger when we planted, fertilized, weeded, and harvested the produce. We grew potatoes, carrots, peas, dill, tomatoes, pumpkins, beans, strawberries, cabbages, lettuces, cucumbers, raspberries, rhubarbs, and corn. We didn't plant vegetables like cauliflower, celery, broccoli, asparagus, pepper, and leek. They weren't a regular part of rural family diets at that time. I didn't try most of those until I was in college. After the produce matured, we cleaned, peeled, diced, and chopped everything to eat immediately or preserve.

As kids, we drank unpasteurized milk, but today, doctors tell us that it's dangerous. Periodically, the US embargoes imported cheese made from unpasteurized milk because of germs like E. coli, listeria, and salmonella. None of our family got raw milk diseases or other illnesses like tuberculosis, diphtheria, typhoid fever, or brucellosis. It may be that the dirt and unsanitary nature of a farm were good for us. Doctors say that children exposed to dirt and animal dander have fewer allergies in adulthood. And we had our fair share of dirt and animal dander. Cows, pigs, and chickens were everywhere, and clouds of dust and dirt surrounded us when we weeded, removed rocks from fields, gathered hay bales, shoveled oats, and cleaned outbuildings. I don't recall ever seeing a cockroach on the farm, but we saw lots of other bugs and spiders. We had no poisonous snakes but lots of black snakes and garter snakes that killed pests like mice.

We even made our own quilts. Grandma Anna and other relatives sometimes came to the farm in the summer to do quilting. They'd sit on the lawn at big rectangular wooden frames that had the underside of the quilt attached by tiny nails. They added a top layer usually decorated with patches and a layer of filler for warmth between. The filler was often a worn blanket. Before electricity, they stitched by hand or used a sewing machine powered by a foot pedal to sew the cloth together to create the patchwork top. They used colorful scraps from old blankets or worn-out clothing cut into squares that they would piece together like a mosaic. By the time I remember watching quilting, electric sewing machines were available and patchwork pieces could be stitched together. Tufted quilts were made by pulling yarn through the quilt and tying a knot to hold the outsides and stuffing of the quilt together. We kids helped some, but mostly we liked to listen to the adult chatter as their big needles went in and out of the fabric, making tufted blankets for our beds. The memories of quilting came back to me many years later when our company sold hand sewn quilts from China.

My first husband represented American textile factories selling to catalogs and department stores. In 1983, my entrepreneurial husband and I traveled to China and spent a month negotiating the production of textile products with the Chinese government because imports were beginning to kill the US textile factories. He decided to join them instead of fighting them to protect his income. That's when American Pacific Enterprises was born. We became one of the early importers, and hand-sewn quilts became one of our most lucrative products.

I couldn't help but think of my ancestors when our business venture ended up a gangbuster success. We sold half a million Chinese quilts to stores and catalogs throughout the US and other countries. But things took a turn when we ran into a public relations problem that involved the Smithsonian. News articles condemned our company for importing handmade quilts and ruining the hobby quilt-maker business.

We had a contract with the Smithsonian Institution in Washington, D.C. to reproduce four historic American quilts they owned and had preserved-an Amish quilt, a Bible quilt, an 1830 design of the Great Seal of the United States, and a bridal quilt. The Smithsonian sold the Chinese reproductions for profit in their museum store, which is not an uncommon revenue source for museums. In one year, they reported over 600,000 dollars in royalties on the quilts.

"Shoddy material! Child labor law abusers! Stealing our business!" Quilter group representatives hated what we were doing. It was a hot-button issue that had quilters' associations coming at us like a swarm of bees. They said that the museum should only accept American goods and that the Chinese work debased theirs. They wanted our quilts to be clearly labeled "Made in China." The quilter organizations started a national campaign to make Congress stop the Smithsonian from selling our quilt products. Over seventy congressional offices had wall-hangings of American-made quilts sent by quilter groups pitching their concerns. The great quilt debate was on.

At this point, our young sons were handling much of the business and weren't sure what to do. That's when they asked me to handle what was becoming a public relations nightmare. I sat at a massive conference table with Smithsonian administrators and about twenty quilter representatives at the museum offices, trying to save our business with the institution. Angry quilter ladies buzzed around my head with accusations and complaints, but I sat stone-faced across from them. Inside, though, I felt conflicted. I could empathize with the hobby quilters who saw beautiful handmade quilts from China being sold for a fraction of the cost of American-made quilts. Quilting is part of our American heritage and is long enjoyed by women, including my ancestors. It was hard for me not to think about those summer days on the lawn when the women in my family gathered to painstakingly create bedding to keep us warm.

We weren't doing anything illegal; we already labeled the quilts "Made in China," and we had a prosperous business we wanted to preserve. But I wanted to mitigate the PR problem by accommodating their concerns as much as possible. I discussed with my sons about increasing the size of the "Made in China" label. Unlike when I planned their European adventure, this time they took my advice. Pressure on the Smithsonian was heavy. Much of their funding comes from Congress. Eventually, they stopped selling our reproduction quilts.

American Pacific had several successes beyond quilts, including importing other home textile products and embroidered jeans and denim jackets and getting hand sewing done for couturiers. Our family import company survived for two generations before being sold in 2001.

Growing up on a farm gave me and my family a sense of self-sufficiency. If we had to, we could plant a garden and raise animals to survive. I could make a quilt to keep us warm. We could recreate the farm that grew the nurturing foods of our childhood. I would learn to live with killing animals like Rosie if it meant our survival. However, I'd prefer not to go back to the days of such hard work. It's the intense labor my family endured for generations that makes me so grateful for the variety and quality of food we can buy today. I never take for granted the great abundance and the many choices in grocery stores. I relish the colorful array of fresh fruits and vegetables, fish markets with so many species, bakeries filled with goodies, and markets with meats from my childhood and kinds I never dreamed of growing up. I'm always thankful for the sweat and blood of all the hardworking people who make our abundant food supply possible.

CHAPTER 16

Old-Time Religion

Our family attended Sunday services at Sacred Heart Church in Stetsonville, Wisconsin. Catholic practices were strict at that time. We weren't allowed to eat meat on Fridays, and we usually only had a fresh fish option in the summer. We relied on canned fish like tuna or salmon or frozen-like-a-rock fish the rest of the year. Most of the time, eating fish was truly a penance. We hated it. Grilled cheese sandwiches were better than the available fish.

The priest conducted the mass in Latin and faced the altar throughout. There was little vocal participation from the pews, but there was plenty of kneeling, standing, and sitting. Masses ran an hour and a half on Sundays, and what seemed to be everlasting sermons was the norm. There we sat, a family of seven, with Dad on the aisle. Since he was usually up before dawn to milk the cows, he often fell asleep to the droning voice of the priest. Mom would poke the closest child, and a chain of pokes went down the line until it was delivered to the last child who poked Dad. Mom then delivered a scowl. Dad would flash a guilty smile.

"Just resting my eyes," he whispered. We all had smirks across our faces when Dad delivered his excuse to Mom.

I enjoyed learning the catechism and participating in the children's choir where we sang old Catholic hymns. They're songs I enjoy and give me peace to this day. When I hear modern singing, the harmonizing, guitar-strummed duets I call "Me 'n' Jesus" songs, I shudder and think about the lovely old reverential hymns in Protestant and Catholic churches in the midtwentieth century. The hymns, the family attendance at mass, the hopeful and loving messages of religion, and the peaceful aura of the church are memories that reinforce my lifelong church affiliation.

All my memories weren't sweet. Sometimes we attended church in Medford where Monsignor Reiter, a crusty old German priest, put the fear of God in me. At the end of mass, he faced the congregation from the altar and gave the same parting words in his heavy German accent. It wasn't an affirming send-off like "Dear parishioners, have a joyful blessed week." It was "Life is short. Death is sure. The hour of death is obscure. One soul you have and only one. When that is lost, all hope is gone." He had me quaking in my shoes. I still shudder when I remember those words! What a message! Fortunately, his was not our parish church, so I didn't have to hear him often.

Women had to wear head covers in the church, so we pinned little circular veils on our heads to pass muster. The priest lectured Mom after mass one Sunday because my veil fell off. I thought it was stupid and petty to reprimand someone on what was an obvious accident and not critical to belief or practices.

When our church needed to raise money, Dad, the township treasurer, met with the banker and the priest to determine pew rental (expected donations) from church members. The priest knew how much money was needed to maintain the church, and who knew more about what people could afford to contribute than the tax collector and the banker? This would not be permitted today due to privacy issues.

My siblings and I went to Catholic summer school in Stetsonville at one of their public schools. It was a requirement in our diocese for children who did not attend Catholic school. The closest Catholic school was ten miles away, and it wasn't possible for us to attend because of transportation and cost.

Catholic nuns who taught summer school wore long black wool habits with starched white cotton hoods covered with black veils. The clothing must have been hot and uncomfortable on summer days in un-air-conditioned class-rooms. There were skinny nuns and fat ones and nice nuns and crabby ones, but no one like Sister Mary Compassionata. That wasn't her name. Whatever it was had nothing to do with compassion. She was stern, seldom smiled, and didn't seem to like children. If she were in a state other than Wisconsin, I bet she would have been handy with a paddle. The kids I knew were usually deterred from misbehavior by an evil stare and threats of being hit on the hands with a ruler. The knuckle-whacking seldom happened. I didn't know until later that kids in other states were disciplined with boards called paddles struck across their buttocks.

I was a teacher-pleaser, so I sat in the front of the class-room close to Sister Mary Compassionata. One morning, boys in the back of the room threw crayons that landed around my feet. I didn't want to get in trouble, so I didn't even look at them. Sister told me to stay after class. "Pick up the crayons," she demanded. I protested that it hadn't been me but the boys who threw them. She scowled at me from under her beaked hood and bleated, "I said, 'Clean them up!'" She treated me like I was a siren from the Odyssey who lured boys into throwing crayons at me! I was angry and thought it was unfair, but I was afraid to complain to the stern, hatchet-faced, black-robed authority. I picked up the crayons and said nothing.

At the time, I didn't have coherent thoughts about the event being a teaching lesson on the subservient role of women, but I recognized the unfair treatment. I thought of it in more expansive terms as an adult. In the Catholic church, women cannot be priests. In recent years, US bishops investigated nuns for spending too much time on societal issues like poverty rather than working to stop abortion. In a broader societal context, I observed that women are more likely to face consequences for acts that men get away with and women are expected to act as the moral compass in relationships. Women are expected to clean up messes made by men like I did with the crayons.

In my young adult years, women who went to Catholic priests for help with spousal abuse were often told not to press their husband's hot buttons and to pray more. Women were essentially told to endure the assaults from their husbands and wait for special recognition in heaven. Psychology studies suggest that domestic abuse damages the mental and physical health of both women and children. Much harm was done by such advice given by priests.

Misogyny goes on. A shortage of priests has led the bishops to discuss allowing married deacons to serve as priests even though the bishops have long held that for a priest to be married would lead to conflicts of interest. Are married deacons more qualified than nuns? Sister Compassionata made a strong impression on me that women are inferior in the eyes of the church.

CHAPTER 17

Worries and Fears

Religion provided solace, but it didn't keep us from fretting about our parents quarreling. We often heard Mom and Dad arguing after we were in bed. Mom always found fault with Dad and his family and harangued him for hours. She complained that neighbors were unkind to her or that they were taking advantage of him. Dad seldom responded. It was hard to stop Mom when she felt wronged. These periods of fighting would calm down for a while but would arise again when Mom perceived some new slight.

Lynda said she has no idea how Dad lived until he was ninety-three. She said, "Dad often didn't get to sleep until two or three in the morning—Mom's time to fight. Then he was up again a few hours later to milk the cows and head to Hurd Manufacturing to work at the mill until it was time to come home and milk the cows again, mend fences, and take care of other chores. Never once did we hear him complain—though he yawned a lot! His patience was extraordinary."

We shuddered whenever we heard raised voices. We worried that they would get divorced and wondered what would happen to us.

World War II was scary. I was not yet in school when the war against Germany was declared in 1941. I had vivid nightmares of German soldiers carrying rifles and racing through the cornfield to burn down our house. A letter from a relative in Europe told of such a thing happening in their town, and of course, as children, we were sure that it could happen to us. I avidly listened to Walter R. Murrow, my favorite radio announcer, for news of progress in the war.

Mom's brother, Alex, was a soldier in three European campaigns during the war, and we tried our best to keep track of where he was or had been through his letters. I remember him as a sad, quiet man with a sweet smile and yellow fingers from smoking unfiltered cigarettes. When he came to visit, Dad tried on his army clothes for a photo. Alex survived the war and came home with a German war bride, Kate, who taught us to sing Christmas songs in German. He died from throat cancer, perhaps from smoking or from working with asbestos at an Illinois roofing company after the war.

For the first time, the US used a nuclear bomb to attack Hiroshima and Nagasaki. Soon after, bomb drills began in schools, and we'd have to get into position by kneeling under our desks with our hands clutched around our heads. I was about nine years old and thought that it was unlikely that bombs would find their way across the ocean and target our country school. I did as I was told, but I did it with a touch of skepticism.

Everything from sugar and coffee to fuel and clothing was rationed to make goods for the war. We kids were too little to miss most of the rationed items like silk and nylon stockings with seams up the back. Most silks came from Japan, so they were unavailable; and nylon was needed to make parachutes. People received coupons for rationed items, allowing only so much for each person. Farmers received extras, so we gave the coupons for gas and tires to relatives who needed them. Butter, cheese, and jams were rationed, but we had plenty on the farm. You couldn't even buy a new car because metal was used for ships, tanks, and jeeps. Everything went to the war effort. The 4-H clubs even collected scrap metal and rubber for the war. The war was scary, and we were so glad when it was over.

We worried about our farm animals and what would happen to them. All the farm animals—cows, chickens, and pigs—had babies. They were our pets, at least for a short time. We learned how to take care of them. Births of baby animals were awesome and exciting events. Every new calf had to be weaned from its mother. The calf had to be taught to drink from a pail rather than from its mother's udder so they wouldn't bond and the mother's milk could be sold. We had to separate them. That was so hard to do. We could see how much they wanted to be together.

There were semiwild barn cats whose job was to keep mice and rats out of the barn. At milking time, they hungrily appeared for a bowl of milk to supplement their protein diets. I never knew how they lived and died outside the barn. I didn't ask questions when I knew the answers would bother me.

The little pigs were noisy, intelligent, and curious. They were lovable. I cringe at the memories of pigs freshly killed—some whose ears I remembered scratching the day before—shot in the head, and hung upside down from hooks ready for the sharp knives that carved them into food packages for the winter. A great aunt made blood sausage from newly killed animals. I watched the blood boiling on her stove as the first step in sausage-making and gagged. Mom chopped chickens' heads off with an ax on a tree stump. They flopped around, headless, spraying blood and dying. She plopped them into a tub and poured boiling hot water on them to clean them and make it easier to pull out their feathers. We pulled out their feathers and laid them out for mom to gut. They were served at dinner later in the day.

Animals died of natural causes, and they were killed for food. The calves were usually sold at two weeks for veal. Older cows, like Rosie, were sent away to become pet food, hamburger, or glue. The lessons in life and death added to our book of life.

I put to death our Labrador Retriever, Jessie, when I was an adult. She was old and ill with heart disease. Our vet told me the end was near. I kept prolonging euthanizing her until one night, when I was walking her, she couldn't get up and breathed with great labor. My sons were grown and out of the house, and my husband was out of town. I took Jessie to an overnight vet who euthanized her while I held her, cried, and thanked her for how much she meant to us. I had her cremated and took her cremains to the river near our house where she always ran to swim. Labradors love water. I smiled when I remembered her taking a running leap over a three-foot privacy fence on our property to head for a swim. As I shook her cremains along the riverbank, I said, "There you go, Jessie. This was always where you wanted to be."

Killing an animal, even if it is to end pain, is torturous. It felt a bit more humane to take time to thank her, to recognize that it is natural to die, and to give her a peaceful death. Buddhists reassure a dying person by relating the good deeds they have done and the good karma accumulated. In the months before she died, I tried to share with

Mom good memories of her and her accumulated good deeds. She had had many wonderful attributes including the way she faced death, with the help of hospice, in a brave and realistic manner. She appreciated having family enumerating her accomplishments.

The killing of Rosie was one of the saddest events of my life. Rosie's death and the killing of animals on the farm were an important reason for my leaving.

CHAPTER 18

Lucky to Survive

When our maternal grandfather, George Milles, was in his early nineties, I asked him how he'd lived so long. He answered, "Stay away from doctors!" He had good reasons for his thinking.

Grandpa was born in the mid-nineteenth century when the average life expectancy was around forty years. People only went to doctors if they were at death's door. Cholera and tuberculosis (TB), smallpox, diphtheria, and typhoid epidemics still occurred. Medicines were ineffective, and Grandpa wanted to avoid common medical procedures like leeches, laxative purgation, and bloodletting to remove impurities from the body. Surgeries were gruesome events with intolerable pain, and few people survived because of blood poisoning. Hospitals were dirty places, and doctors still believed that bad air, not germs, caused illness.

By the time my parents were born in 1915 and 1916, medical care had improved, but the average life span was still only 52.5 years for males and 56.8 years for females. Roughly 10 percent of infants died during their first year. More than 20 million people died in the 1918 influenza pandemic—one of the deadliest disease outbreaks in history. TB (also called consumption) marred their childhoods. It was common for neighbors and friends to die from the hideous disease. By the beginning of the twentieth century, doctors understood the causes of TB, but it still killed a lot of people in the United States. It affected many young people, and I recall Mom pointing out a farm where children who died from TB were buried.

I was born in 1936 when the projected average life span for a woman was 60.6 years. By then, medical care had advanced. Louis Pasteur's discoveries led to an understanding that germs caused illnesses, the use of ether as an anesthetic made surgery bearable, and surgical outcomes improved.

Our doctors and the closest hospital were ten miles away in Medford. When I was a child, it was a proprietary hospital, which meant the doctors owned it. It had thirty-four beds, an operating room, a delivery room, a couple of ward rooms, several private rooms, and an X-ray machine used to set bone fractures in the basement. Before the invention of the X-ray, doctors reset fractures by feel. X-rays were a great help in making their work more accurate.

Invented in the 1890s, X-rays allowed doctors to see bones, organs, kidney stones, accidentally swallowed objects, bullets, and even cancer. When we were children, doctors used X-rays for various medical purposes. My sister Barbara and I had X-rays done when we were in our teens to kill stubborn plantar warts on our feet. A big scope was placed over the warts, and an electric switch sent radiation into our feet to destroy them. In the thirties and forties, the person who administered X-rays at the hospital also drove doctors to home births and administered analgesics. Often these people had no formal training but were indispensable to the doctors. I don't remember that technicians or doctors took special precautions to protect themselves or that they draped us with lead coverings to prevent radiation from going into surrounding tissues.

Our younger sister Lynda said, "I had multiple X-rays on my throat. Finally, I had my tonsils and adenoids removed." We were in the generation that experienced a medical zeal for the new tool of radiation. It was used for numerous problems like adenoid and sinus and inner-ear problems. X-ray examinations in those days had a large beam and exposed much more of the patient's anatomy than was necessary. The practices at that time frighten radiation experts today.

Shoe stores had X-ray machines in big wooden boxes called shoe-fitting fluoroscopes. We'd put a foot in a hole in the bottom of the box and look through a viewer. "Whee! Look at that! I can see the bones in my feet." We could see how much room we had in our shoes. My brother David remembers leaving his feet inside the machine for a long time, mesmerized by the view. He says, "I still count my toes after a shower to make sure I didn't grow more toes as a result of my infatuation with fluoroscopes."

Polio, a viral infection of the spinal cord, was a specter in my childhood because the disease targeted mostly children. Many children died or were left with paralyzed arms and legs. Aching limbs or fevers were alarming to our parents, and fears of catching polio kept us away from movie theaters and crowds. A neighbor boy, Dennis, developed polio, and we prayed every night that we wouldn't get it. Dennis made a full recovery, no credit to my brother David and his friend who made Dennis trip and break his crutches. "There was hell to pay at home for me and my friend over that," David remembers.

Children with polio who lost the ability to breathe on their own were often put in big cylindrical metal capsules called iron lungs, which provided respiration. With only the head and neck sticking out, air pressure was reduced and increased to simulate breathing. Some people lived for years in such a state.

As children, we proudly donated to the March of Dimes, an organization founded by President Franklin D. Roosevelt in 1938 as the National Foundation for Infantile Paralysis to combat polio. We put dimes in charity boxes or cards with slots to help fund polio prevention and treatment. The Sister Kenny Institute was founded in 1942, and it treated polio patients throughout the US at a Minnesota facility. Today, the March of Dimes works to prevent premature birth and to promote the wellness of infants and mothers.

The Salk vaccine, which targets polio, became available in 1955 when I was already a teen. My first inoculation was a shot. A few years later, children, including my younger siblings, got the oral vaccine Sabin developed that was administered as a sugar cube soaked in the vaccine, cheaper to make and easier to administer than the vaccine shot I had. Today, vaccines have eliminated polio in the US and most countries of the world.

When I was about eight or nine years old, I spent two weeks in the Medford Hospital. I had pneumonia in both lungs that may have stemmed from a bout with the flu. The antibiotic penicillin was discovered in 1928 and used in the military but was not widely used until after 1945. I was probably given the antibacterial drug *sulfa* in the hospital.

A traveling research doctor who was trying to develop a vaccine for pneumonia asked my parents if he could take blood samples while I was in the hospital. He used different needles to try to draw blood, but he was unsuccessful. He told my dad I had rolling veins. Upon hearing that my veins were on the move, my tough dad, who could calmly kill and butcher animals, walked into the hall and fainted. As an adult, I still shiver at the thought of having blood drawn, although phlebotomists have told me that the research doctor was inept at drawing blood.

Around the age of ten, I cut my leg on a piece of metal sticking out on a car. The cut was deep and required suturing. If the doctors administered anesthetic, it didn't help. The stitching may have begun before I was numb. I could feel the needle puncture my flesh over and over. It took two nurses and my parents to hold me down on a gurney while the doctor sewed the large gash while I screamed. I have a four-inch-long, half-inch-wide scar on my knee. When doctors see it and ask what happened to me, I shrug it off and say that I came from a farm community where the best surgeons were vets. Obviously, I didn't have a veterinary surgeon!

I had my appendix taken out when I was eleven. The drive to the hospital in Medford was excruciating. It seemed we hit every bump in the road and drove over every set of uneven railroad track in the county. Each time Dad's car hit rough terrain, I screamed and, each curve he took on the country road caused me to screech. I was certain that my small frame and inflamed appendix weren't going to survive the ride. When we made it to the tiny hospital, the surgeon placed a funnel over my nose and mouth to anesthetize me. I breathed in the sickening-smelling ether, counted backward from ten, and awoke with a wide scar on my abdomen where the doctor had plucked the infected organ from my body.

Medical care was cheap, at least in comparison to today. In the early 1950s, there was a lot of rheumatic fever, which caused a form of arthritis and heart valve disease. This is a 1954 bill from such a patient:

Hospital, 11 days 66.00
Drugs 10.40
Professional Services,
W.W. Meyer, M.D. 25.00
$113.90 total

We had no yearly wellness exams or preventative care at a pediatrician's office when I was a child. However, it's likely that a combined vaccine for diphtheria, tetanus, and pertussis was available in my early childhood, and I'm sure we were vaccinated. We'd only see a doctor if we were sick. Otherwise, Mom took care of us with various remedies. We used aspirin for aches and pains, and a greasy, strong ointment called Vicks VapoRub for colds and coughs. Mom would put it on our chests or drop dollops of the camphor-smelling gel into bowls of hot water and have us hang our heads draped with towels over the steaming medicated water and inhale. The treatment made us cough heartily.

Sanitation was a problem in the early 1900s; but hospitals were becoming cleaner, and doctors encouraged families to bathe more than once a week, wash their hands, and maintain cleanliness while working around food. When we got indoor plumbing and bathed often, Grandpa George told us that it was going to dry out our skin. We learned our cleanliness lessons so well that my husband named my sisters and me the "Bleach Babes." I bleach linens and cupboards and am always grousing about his failure to sterilize the cutting board and failing to clean the kitchen to my hygienic standards.

Mom tried to follow advice from doctors and decided that we should eat calf liver because physicians said it was healthy. We all hated the tough, slimy meat drowned in fried onions. The smell of it cooking on the stove almost made me faint. I thought it was disgusting to eat an organ that sifted poisons out of our blood. I would have run away if I had to eat brains or intestines. It sounded cannibalistic. What we would have given for our dog to be inside during dinner to help us out. Instead, we went the route of tucking small pieces of liver into big pieces of bread so we didn't have to taste it. Another go-to to avoid the repulsive dinner was to tuck it in our pockets and take it to our dog as soon as we were out of Mom's line of sight.

Barbara received the Sarah Bernhardt Acting Award from her siblings for throwing up on the dining room table and putting an end to the forced consumption of liver. I never lost my aversion for the awful meat, yet I fed my sons butter-fried chicken livers. I look back and am amazed that I made my children endure things I hated as a child. I couldn't stand the smell as I lifted a forkful of the supposedly healthy meat on it toward my boys' mouths, but I'd cheerily chirp, "Open up. An airplane is coming into the hanger."

Because we had a big family, we kept two dentists busy. I don't know who the younger kids went to, but the older kids and Mom and Dad went to an older, well-regarded dentist in Medford. I believe he was the president of the Wisconsin Dental Society at one time. I was scared to death of him. He couldn't have been more than five feet tall; but he had a bristling demeanor, and he projected authority and anger. I heard him yelling profanities at some poor patient while I waited with trepidation for him to look at my teeth. I shut my eyes, and he was suddenly standing next to me. I almost jumped out of the chair.

He scared my sister Lynda and told her, "No braces for you! You don't need braces any more than a pig needs two tails." Instead of braces, he told her to push her front tooth forward with her finger day and night because it was growing in crooked. Her finger was always in her mouth. The dental Nazi's finger method straightened her pearly whites.

We switched to a dentist in Dorchester for a time when I was about twelve, one who gave the new treatment of topical fluoride on our teeth. It was probably too late for me, but they may have helped my younger siblings. I have been a dentist's annuity with lots of fillings and dental procedures throughout my life. Once my parents' generation aged, they ended up with false teeth or bridges. Poor Mom had to glue in her partial plate of false teeth when she went out, which restricted what she could eat. Dad had all his teeth pulled and got dentures. They didn't fit, and the grouchy dentist said he'd have to live with them. Dad threw them on his desk and said they were going to be fixed. They were.

Children today have healthier, straighter teeth because of fluoride in water, improved dental care, electric toothbrushes, toothpaste, and braces. I doubt many kids can say they used their finger to fix a crooked tooth. Older people of my generation use root canals and implants to continue to eat and look well by keeping our natural teeth. One of my granddaughters is going off to college without ever having a cavity. Isn't she lucky?

CHAPTER 19

Elsie from Chelsea

I was in fifth grade when I saw an article in the Medford *Star News* that a woman in Chelsea, a nearby village, had been arrested for keeping a "disorderly house." I headed straight to Dad, who was my primary source of information. The headline shocked me, and I asked him, "Can a person be arrested for not keeping a clean house?" It was the most absurd thing I ever heard. Everyone's house was messy from time to time, including ours. He hemmed and hawed for a moment and looked away, seeming to grasp for words. He quietly said, "Ask your mother." I knew then it was a taboo subject and didn't pursue it. I didn't realize a disorderly house meant something indecent or corrupt was going on, and I couldn't look up "disorderly house" or "Elsie from Chelsea" on the internet. I didn't connect the story to little joking asides by adults about "Elsie from Chelsea." Much later I learned that Elsie from Chelsea was doing something indecent that had nothing to do with dirty dishes or dusty furniture. We learned not to ask questions about sex. We were naïve kids and were afraid to push boundaries of adult comfort.

Any questions from children were greeted with vague answers or ignored. Sex education wasn't taught in schools, and talk of it was minimal in our house. The closest we came to "the talk" was when Mom gave Barbara and me some pamphlets she'd gotten from a sanitary napkin company. We were in seventh or eighth grades. The pamphlets had vague information that wasn't helpful, but we didn't ask questions. What we didn't gain from the feminine products literature, we got from the farm. We had ample opportunities to observe sex among our farm animals.

While the cows, pigs, and chickens gave us a basic idea of how it occurred, all I gathered from watching their mating activities was the males, snorting and grunting, appeared to enjoy it heartily; but the females seemed scared and unenthusiastic. We had a lot to learn about the mechanics, biology, and even the language of sex. We didn't know what *gay* meant except "fun, carefree, or lighthearted."

Same sex couples weren't on our radar, and LBGT pride parades were decades away. We used words like *fairies* or *queers* but didn't really know what they meant. We knew it wasn't approved behavior. Homosexuality was considered a disease and not something to talk about. We had an older male cousin who liked to bake and style his mother's hair. We thought it was odd, but adults didn't talk about it. Barbara remembers she and her high school friends often went to a boy's house for lunch. His mom was away at work, so he and the girls could smoke and laugh. She said he was fun and like one of the girls. No one made fun of him or used gay slurs in talking about him. She also remembers seeing posted college dorm rules that said two girls could not sleep together. "I wondered why anyone would want to share the tiny bunks. I didn't figure out until later that the sign had nothing to do with overcrowding of bunks," she says, recognizing her naivety.

My brother, David, does not remember thinking anyone was gay in high school. "The subject never came up. I don't think those who were gay wanted to differentiate themselves," he said. When he attended his fiftieth high-school reunion, the valedictorian of his class introduced him to her female spouse. "So," he said, "they were out there, even in Medford." Our naivete kept us in the dark, and our insular society kept them in the closet.

CHAPTER 20

Reading and 'Riting and 'Rithmetic

Lawndale Elementary

We learned reading and writing and arithmetic in a one-room rural school a mile and a half from our farm. Unlike the words in the old song, "reading, 'riting, and 'rithmetic taught to the tune of the hickory stick," no hickory sticks or wooden paddles were used in our classroom. David, Barbara, and I went to paddle-free Lawndale Elementary from first through eighth grade. We were threatened with a ruler a few times, but Wisconsin was not a big paddling state, a gift from our progressive German and Scandinavian settlers.

When we were kids, kindergarten wasn't available in our community, so school began in the first grade. However, I got a taste of school at age five after memorizing the poem "A Visit from St. Nicholas" by Clement Clarke Moore. My proud parents told the teacher, and she put me in the school's Christmas performance. I was ecstatic! I believed in Santa Claus, and the year before, as my sister Barbara and I lay sleepless in our beds the night before Christmas, we heard reindeer on the roof over our bedroom. Santa would be coming to visit soon. I was excited and honored to recite Moore's words. I stood on the stage, a small wood platform balanced on cement blocks, to recite the poem. I was dressed in my very best Sunday dress and shoes. I said the poem without prompting from the teacher or Mom and Dad. I took a little bow and smiled at my parents who were so proud of me. I had a good feeling about being in school and couldn't wait until fall when I would be there.

That fall, Miss Lemke, the same teacher who cast me in the Christmas program, became my first-grade teacher. I was smitten from day one. She opened my world when she taught me to read stories about Dick and Jane, their dog Spot, and baby Sally. The books were not hardbound but more like booklets. We read, "See Dick go. Go, Dick, go."

It was fun to read them aloud. There was a lot of repetition and illustrations that helped us understand the story. We didn't have books at our reading level at home. This was my introduction to reading. To this day, I think fondly of Miss Lemke and Dick and Jane.

Lawndale Elementary was a small wooden structure when Grandma Anna Ludwig (nee Fritsche) attended it in the late 1800s. It burned down and was replaced by a brick building that my dad, older siblings, and I all attended through eighth grade. Like my dad and his mother, we walked to school since there was no school bus. We made the journey through ice and snow except for occasions when my generation might catch a ride with a milk truck. If we turned around and went home because we were cold, Mom and Dad's response was "Put on another pair of pants or heavy wool stockings and get going." Pity was hard to come by, even in subzero Wisconsin.

I visited the school around 2003. It appeared that the less than 3,000 square-foot building that was once a place of learning had become a storage spot for hay bales. It continues to remain standing but barely. Knee-high weeds grow around the building, and it appears to be unused. Even though its use changed, it was easy for me to imagine the one-story rectangular building exactly as it had been so many years ago.

The small school shoehorned forty to sixty students of different ages and grades into a small space. We entered through a cloakroom where we would hang our coats and leave our snowy boots. On each side of the cloakroom were storage rooms. I remember piling wood that fueled the furnace. The other room stored books and supplies.

I came in the school quietly each day as was required and slid into my student desk made of oak with cast-iron legs. Desks were arranged by grade and faced the north wall. A table with small chairs and a teacher's desk were on the north side. Chalkboards were on the wall behind the teacher's desk. Over them were white strips of paper with examples of Palmer penmanship cursive writing that we were to use as a guide in our written work. We learned cursive writing when we were about eight and were graded on our report cards on how well we made cursive letters.

Two bookcases of books in the southwest corner constituted our entire library. We read every book before we got to the fourth grade. A print of Gilbert Stuart's *George Washington* painting hung on the wall above the teacher's desk. I smiled every time I looked at the image because he looked like my paternal grandfather's sister-in-law, Ella, in Oshkosh. Her gray, frizzy hair stuck out on the sides of her head like the first American president.

A furnace that took up the northwest corner of the room was lit and stoked by the teacher to warm the room before students arrived. Students were responsible for keeping the room tidy during the day, but our teacher cleaned the room before and after school. The older kids had room assignments like going to the outdoor pump house to get buckets of water before school started. I hated going out in icy cold weather to get water. One bucket had a dipper for drinking at the entrance of school. Another bucket held water brought in for handwashing.

Bathroom breaks didn't mean we got a hall pass that allowed us to roam around and wave at friends in different classrooms. With one main room and no indoor plumbing, going to the bathroom meant a trek to the two-seater outhouses. They were freezing cold in winter, odoriferous always, and often filled with spiderwebs. There was one for girls and one for boys, and on cold, wintry days, the walks were dreadful. They were not places to linger, and I made sure my trips were short.

A hot lunch program and a cafeteria with tables and chairs would have thrilled us. Instead, we ate cold leftovers from the night before or peanut butter sandwiches at our desks. We stored our syrup container lunch buckets in the icy cloakroom, and sometimes our sandwiches froze if we forgot to bring them in to thaw. We considered it a lucky day when we'd get cookies Mom made or a Fig Newton.

Our teacher walked up and down the rows of seats before we ate with a pitcher of soapy water and poured warm suds over our hands to clean them. I don't know if it was the not-so-tasty lunches or the vast amount of walking and farmwork, but I don't recall any overweight kids.

My brothers had to sit at the front of the classroom in the early grades because they were restless, but I was one of the older kids the teachers liked. I helped teachers correct papers and teach small groups or individuals. But even though I was well-liked and enjoyed helping doesn't mean I was a goody, goody Pearl Pureheart, the sweetest cartoon mouse in all of Disneyland Micedom. I had a bit of an ornery streak despite wanting to be a good student and liked by my teacher.

We were supposed to be silent, working at our desks, unless we were talking to the teacher or helping another student. The too-quiet classroom gave me an itch to stir up some noise. To my delight, I discovered I could turn the radio on full volume and still have enough time to get back to my desk to sit and appear studious. I'd have my nose buried in a book by the time it warmed up enough to blast sound and disturb the students and teacher. My stealth maneuvers and mischief thrilled me. Mr. Wall eventually caught on and threatened to hit my hands with a ruler. Being helpful in school, plus having Dad on the school board, gave us a little leeway when we misbehaved. My hands were never smacked; however, I did give up the radio game.

Another way of creating noise and a little chaos was the use of caps (paper strips embedded with bits of gunpowder). We brought them in rolls to school and put them at the joint where desk seats were attached to the frame. They would explode when an unsuspecting student sat down. I liked having fun, but one prank I didn't take part in was putting thumbtacks on the teacher's chair. When I did take part in mischief, I was usually far away when the ensuing trouble erupted.

Barbara, David, and I planned a prank that could have gotten us in real trouble. We decided to stuff a raw potato in Mr. Wall's car tailpipe during one of our long recesses. David was the lookout, while Barbara and I took turns shoving it in. We congratulated ourselves that we didn't get caught. Barbara belatedly figured out that Mr. Wall might die of carbon monoxide poisoning from the stuffed tailpipe. We grew very nervous. "What if the police find our fingerprints? We weren't thinking. We should have worn gloves." At the ripe ages of eight, ten, and twelve, we'd surely face murder charges! We shuddered to think of the consequences and waited for something bad to happen. Each day that Mr. Wall was at school was pure relief. We looked at one another and smiled when we entered his classroom. No mention was ever made of our attempt to take out a teacher.

One-room schools had a poor teacher-pupil ratio. My youngest brother, Lin, said, "My class didn't meet often. There was only one other kid in my grade, and the teacher hardly ever brought us up to the table for instruction. There were more than forty kids and eight grades to teach. Too many kids in too many grades for one teacher to give attention to everyone all the time. I listened to other classes to learn, and I oversaw the science lab kit and played with that during school," he explained.

Like most country schools, our school's teachers were mostly women, young and poorly paid. Lin recalls, "One thing that sticks in my mind about Lawndale was my third-grade teacher, Allen Kalman. Mr. Kalman was a good teacher and seemed to like his job but left teaching for a meat-cutting job to make enough money to support his family. He then left that job to become a sailor on the Great Lakes for better pay. Unfortunately, he had just taken a job on the Edmund Fitzgerald when the ship sank with all hands in Lake Superior, November 10, 1975. He had been a sailor for two weeks."

Teachers had the heavy responsibility of overseeing the health, safety, and education of kids. It's no surprise that the burnout rate was so high. I don't remember having a teacher for more than a year. Most teachers were graduates of two-year teacher-training institutions called normal schools. The normal schools, which later became teacher colleges, trained teachers in reading, math, character building, and discipline. But despite their training, teaching forty to sixty children in eight different grades was challenging. Teachers spent their days battling students who were reluctant learners and trying to teach others who had unidentified learning problems they were unprepared to handle. There were no special education classes or tutoring programs, so they failed students who didn't learn at grade level as some did repeatedly. We had some teenage third and fourth graders.

We had a lot of freedom. In warm weather, teachers let us play baseball or take nature walks in the woods behind the school for most of the day. It was a great thing to do in the spring when wildflowers were in bloom. We'd pick yellow mayflowers, white lady's slippers, white trilliums, buttercups, violets, and bluebells, which we would bring back to the classroom for the teacher. We played baseball for hours in the spring and fall. Male teachers also led football games for the older boys. I remember a teacher telling us, "If you see a maroon car parked on the road next to the playground, hurry into school and sit down." A couple of children were assigned to sit on the steps and watch for the car as the games went on all afternoon. That car meant a visit from the county teaching supervisor.

At Halloween, the upper grades planned scary surprises and decorated the wood storage room to turn it into a spook house. Younger kids would walk through the darkened room, and we tried to terrify them with our screams, flashlights, and costumes. At Christmas, we created a stage made of planks on the floor and did a Christmas show for parents. It was mostly us singing Christmas songs, but Santa would end the event by showing up with bags of popcorn and candy. He'd shout out, "Have you all been good boys and girls this year?" We yelled at the top of our lungs, "Yes!" That show was especially exciting because it meant Christmas vacation was coming and Santa would come down our chimney soon. In some communities, teachers were judged by the Christmas show, and their next year's contract was decided by how well the pageant was conducted.

Barb and I had our brother David believing in Santa Claus until he was ten years old. David jokes about this and says, "When I started to reach the age where I doubted if there was a Santa Claus or the Easter Bunny, my older sisters Nadine and Barbara kept reassuring me that they were real. I think I was almost shaving before I learned the truth." His friends told him otherwise, but Barb and I swooped in and said, "Who are you going to believe, your sisters or your dumb friends?" He was wise to go with his loving sisters. We were the girls who terrorized boys who might tease him or try to fight with him. Barbara sees a rosier world than I and claims that we weren't being mean girls but were trying to prolong his childhood. It might have been a little of both.

I loved reading about history. We had to be quiet and orderly in school, and reading was an enjoyable way to be so. In upper elementary grades, I checked out books about WWII and Russia from the Medford Library. Since Russia and the US were antagonistic forces after WWII, I wanted to know more about our communist enemy, and I went on a Russian history book reading kick. There were so many great WWII books. My favorite author was John Hersey, and a couple of my favorite books were *The Wall* and *A Bell for Adano*. I still love reading, and I belong to two book clubs—one primarily fiction and the other nonfiction. I like real books made of pulp and ink that you can touch and page through, not a digital device that you use your finger to scroll through the prose. You will not find a Kindle in my house. Instead, you will find my bedside stand with a tall stack of books, waiting to be read.

My younger brother and sister, Lin and Lynda, went to consolidated schools and did not have the one-room schoolhouse experience. Consolidated schools were being promoted as education reform because they brought cost efficiency and an expanded curriculum. Some people lamented losing the one-room school, which brought families from a small community together for social activities like the Christmas program and the last day of school picnic. Education reform won. The one-room schools in Wisconsin and elsewhere almost ceased to exist after 1960.

We didn't find school demanding. We never fussed about homework because it was seldom assigned. Most farmers at that time didn't want their children bothered with homework because children's labor was essential on a farm. We didn't worry about our academic rank among peers. When I was growing up, I was unaware of any ranking of school districts by the state or newspapers or magazines. We didn't have television, social media, or the internet to compare ourselves to others. It would have been considered boastful to talk about academic successes. It was a different world compared to what I saw my children go through.

When my children were young, homework was a nightly ritual during middle school and high school. We'd spend many nights together sitting at the kitchen table until almost midnight, working subject by subject to complete the homework. They did rigorous preparation for junior and senior high school academic testing programs like the ACT and SAT to get the scores needed to get into good colleges.

I think I had more fun in school than my children or grandchildren. We had more carefree schooltime. I didn't learn much history, math, or science, which I regret, but anyone who wants to learn has a lifetime to do that. Public libraries were there to extend the small library in my one-room school. The younger children in our family had regular deliveries of books from the Medford Library in their schools. We felt important and useful because we helped little schoolchildren learn. It was an extension of our home where we learned to be responsible for others. We kept our schoolroom orderly and clean because we were responsible for the custodial duties just as we were at home.

Compared to schools today, Lawndale Elementary didn't stack up well in academic preparation. It certainly didn't produce any Fulbright scholars. My classmates at Lawndale Elementary didn't talk about going to college. Children grew up, married, and remained on farms or worked nearby at the feed mill, window manufacturing company, cheese factory, mink farm, gas station, roadbuilding company, or the wood products company. For most people in our community, it was a completely acceptable education. Children learned to get along with others, to look out for others, to follow rules, to settle disagreements, to work carefully, and to be obedient. Our school prepared students to be successful where we lived, not where some of us wanted to go which required more academic experience.

We understood there were broader vistas for learning than our small school. My brothers and sisters and I were ambitious and had a bit of gumption. We would not settle for an abbreviated education or staying in a place with limited opportunities.

CHAPTER 21

High School—Finally a Path Is Chosen

In August of 1954, I moved from our one-room elementary school to Medford High School. I was thirteen years old, weighed eighty-five pounds, and stood five feet tall when I boarded the school bus. When I stepped off the bus ten miles from home and came face-to-face with the next four years of my life, I was met with 190 other freshmen and hundreds more upperclassmen bustling through the crowded hallways. I was terrified.

This transition wasn't smooth or comfortable. Since Mom rarely shared anything about her teen years and Dad didn't go to school beyond the eighth grade, I wasn't given any insights from my parents. I assume they didn't know what to tell me. I was on my own to figure out the lay of the land and how to survive in this unknown territory.

With only a vague idea of what courses I would take and even less knowledge about how to navigate the halls and unfamiliar faces, my freshman year was a shock. I walked in wearing my hand-sewn clothes and feeling scared, dizzy, disoriented, and shrimpy small for my age. I was certain that the other kids were smarter and saw me as a country bumpkin. But as the oldest child, I knew I was paving the way for my siblings, and I had better take hold of my fears and dig in.

There was no new-school walk-through with parents like what my grandchildren usually have, but I meandered through the vast building and found my way to each class. I knew I was there to work hard, not get in trouble, and prepare for the next step—college or work—but I had no idea what I wanted to do. I had few models for careers, and since there was no money for college or encouragement from home, it seemed that heading off to a university was not in my future.

During the first semester of my freshman year, I learned that my math skills weren't up to par. It wasn't much of a surprise since my elementary teachers weren't math whizzes themselves. But when my algebra teacher asked me to work through algebraic calculations in a class filled with high school juniors and seniors, I felt myself drowning in variables and exponents. I scored in the top ten among two hundred or so students on the Taylor County eighth grade exams. Teachers probably expected more of me. What they didn't realize is that my true gifts were advanced knowledge of recess games and teaching little kids how to read. Besides, I didn't really see any use for algebra in my world.

The algebra teacher, Mr. Retzer, said we were the dumbest kids he'd ever taught. He was an ex-military man and had a demanding authority and slashing sarcasm that scared me. I guess he thought that criticism would make us work harder. All it did was scare me to death. I feared he'd reprimand me, so I took a seat in the back row. The days of sitting in the front of the class and being the teacher's pet seemed to be far behind me. I hunkered down at my desk to shield myself from his tirades. After receiving a D on the first grading period, I was propelled to work hard. I wanted to make sure everyone knew that I wasn't to be written off as another kid who couldn't make it. I took serious efforts to overcome my algebra deficiencies with some help from my dad. Although Dad had never learned algebra, he was able to help me figure out silly logic and math puzzles Mr. Retzer had us solve. I didn't get an A, but I survived.

In our family pioneer days of the late 1800s, Medford, the site of our high school, was a small town with about one thousand people, and over the years, not much has changed. The 1950 Census showed 2,799 residents. The 2010 Census showed a population of 4,326. The area remains around 97 percent Caucasian. The single high school in Medford was built in the 1920s. It is the high school my mother, my two other siblings, and I attended. In 1969, a new school our youngest brother and sister attended was completed, and the high school I attended became a middle school. The new high school is much larger and has a swimming pool. *US News and World Report* (2019) reports the number of students in ninth through twelfth grades was 628, about the same as when I graduated in 1954. The school has a 93 percent graduation rate, about average for the state. I do not recall such record-keeping when I attended Medford High School. I kept in mind Mom's hope that I would be a secretary at the Pfister Hotel and decided to take typing, shorthand, bookkeeping, and a work program to prepare for the business world.

In typing class, I would plunk, plunk, plunk the metal keys of a heavy black manual typewriter. When the bell rang to alert me that I was coming to the end of the line, I would complete the word I was typing and then use the side lever to shift the paper back to the beginning of the next line. Our teacher, Mr. Werz, should have worn ear protectors. A class full of students banging away on manual typewriters was noisy. I could type sixty words a minute, which pleased me, given the laborious process. I became adept at shorthand and could take notes with the best of them using the symbols and abbreviations. It was like writing in a foreign language. Back then, shorthand was a way to provide an accurate record of spoken words. It was a skill needed by secretaries, but today it's probably unknown outside courtrooms where it's used on stenotype machines. I still use some of the symbols when taking notes today.

Once I got the hang of typing and shorthand, I started working at the Rural Electric Association (REA) office a couple afternoons a week as part of my work experience. I loathed typing long papers because mistakes had to be manually corrected through five, six, or more layers of carbon copies. We had to erase the errors on each page by typing the correction on a white correction tape. We also used liquid paper correction fluid to paint over the error and then retype. What a delight it is to get rid of errors on a computer document using backspace or delete buttons.

I soon realized that I didn't share my mom's dream of becoming a secretary. I wanted to go to college. Even though this was out of the ordinary for our family, I signed up for a college prep major. A double major meant little in-school study time and a full course load. My modus operandi was to learn by being the watcher, waiting and hoping I'd figure out what I needed to get into college while trying to look cool.

I made friends easily and always tried to be a good friend. The senior album description of me was "A smiling face and twinkling eye. You simply cannot pass her by." Two of my best friends, Sandy and Barb Kuse, were cousins who lived in Medford. Another friend, Fern Mathey, was a farm girl like me. We sometimes walked to the Medford girls' houses to eat lunch and would stay for sleepovers when there were after school activities. We were best friends throughout high school.

My three closest friends and I were in the high school band. We had fun playing at home and at out-of-town high school football games and in marches for community festivals. I played the clarinet but was the first one with my hand up when Mr. Abrahamson, our director and husband of my 4-H mentor, sought a volunteer to learn snare drums for marches. That seemed far more exciting than looking down my nose at music on the end of the long black clarinet as I marched along. I entered district clarinet contests and was first chair clarinet in the band despite not being that great. My sister Barbara played in the percussion section. She remembers walking into the band room during lunch and seeing a few teachers and coaches enjoying a beer with lunch. She said, "Wisconsin is big beer country, so they may have considered it a healthy lunch."

There were after-school clubs and activities. I loved the modern dance club led by our gym instructor, Miss Jane Pettibone. She taught us to dance with drama using our whole bodies. I'm still a bit of a drama queen in my aerobics dancing. I also had fun with drama of the acting sort. I got a boost when my English teacher, Miss Alberta Thaldorf, suggested I try out for the sophomore class play.

She was the director, and I got the starring role. I guess I had an "in" on that role. Mom and Dad were supportive of our after-school activities even if it inconvenienced them by having to pick us up after school.

I loved history class with Miss Lucille Niland. We read *Time* magazine and talked about world affairs. President Truman had desegregated the military in 1947; but racial problems seemed endemic, and even our little Caucasian farm community took notice. The Supreme Court ruled that segregation in the public schools was unconstitutional (*Brown v. Board of Education of Topeka*, Kansas, 1954). Queen Elizabeth was coronated, Joseph Stalin died, the twenty-second amendment limiting the president to two terms passed, and our Wisconsin senator Joseph McCarthy led hearings on infiltration of communists in the State Department. All these events happened during my high school days. By the time I was in high school, our family had daily and weekly newspapers, which we avidly read about world events. History class was the place we discussed these events. I hoped someday to visit countries like Russia and England. I didn't know anyone in my high school who traveled outside the country, and there were many who hadn't traveled outside the state. We learned about the world from history classes, books, magazines, newspapers, the radio, and now, television, which arrived at home during my high school days.

High school provided a reckoning that others had nicer things, traveled more, and had a better education. Class and money influenced teachers, and they were partial to students whose families were better off. It might have been disheartening if those kids were the majority. Popularity among students depended on being friendly, smart, and talented in some way, and being pretty or handsome helped. Athleticism worked well for boys, but the girls didn't have that option. At noon breaks, girls donned goofy one-piece blue cotton rompers and played intramural basketball. The game required us to stay on a half-court. Maybe they thought girls were too weak to handle a full floor.

Boys asked me on dates or, more often, would tell one of my friends they wanted to date me. They certainly didn't notice me for my feminine endowments. I had not started my growth spurt as a freshman and would not do so until I was fifteen. I was delayed in the puberty department. I grew almost six inches in my sophomore year; Mom and I were lengthening my dresses every few months. Yes, we mostly wore dresses and skirts. We sometimes wore poodle skirts, which were long and had a poodle (or some other animal) applique with voluminous crinoline slips underneath, paired with saddle shoes and bobby socks. By my senior year, jeans became the *in* thing, although we sometimes called them dungarees. They were rolled up and sometimes had leather patches on the pocket. Wearing them was an act of rebellion inspired by movies with James Dean and

Marlon Brando. Adults thought we were going to hell in a handbasket.

I already started to like the attention of boys a few years earlier and thought it would be fun to go on a date. The snag was that my parents said I couldn't date until I was sixteen. Although I wasn't pleased about the rule at the time, in retrospect, it makes sense since I was immature physically and emotionally. Somehow the tables turned for my sister Barb who is seventeen months younger than I am. Mom and Dad allowed her to date as a freshman on the condition that she would double-date with me. Not only could younger siblings do fun things earlier than older ones but the older ones also had to supervise and be responsible for them.

Smart, handsome, dark-haired athletic guys with nice smiles were my type. As a sophomore, I saw a freshman boy who met the attraction test. I told my friends I had a crush on him, and my dear friends followed up. Soon I was regularly dating a great guy for school events. Mike was my special guy throughout high school. Whenever I smell gardenias, I think back to high school proms and the tropical wrist bouquets I received. As we danced, my gardenia-laden wrist came around my boyfriend's neck and gave me its strong but lovely scent. I always break out in a smile when I smell a gardenia flower in a garden shop or flower market. I loved dancing to songs by Frank Sinatra, Eddie Fisher, and Perry Como. We crooned along to "Secret Love" and "Stranger in Paradise" and sang silly ones like "How Much Is that Doggie in the Window?" Bill Haley and the Comets had just come along and introduced us to the beginning of rock and roll with "Rock around the Clock." Not many guys in our HS danced to that music. The girls danced together. Elvis Presley would soon follow.

Mike and I were two Catholic kids, ingrained with Catholic education about proper behavior. Catholic education about sex was nonexistent, and the advice was to hold off on sexual bliss until marriage. Parents did little to help in helping us negotiate love, and sex was a land mine subject, at least at my house. The relationship was chaste. I didn't want to end up a pregnant teen like my mom. I wasn't about to have my hopes and dreams smashed and end up stuck on a farm or in a small town for the rest of my life. Boys could call me ice queen if they wanted, but living my life on my terms was more important to me than some high school amorous adventures. I was resolute.

An exciting milestone for most teenagers is learning to drive, unless you grow up driving tractors. For me, learning to drive wasn't a big deal or a daunting experience. By the time I started high school, Dad let me drive home from church on Sundays when Mom didn't attend. He'd sit in the passenger seat, perusing the Sunday paper, as my brothers and sisters tormented me from the back seat. I did my best to deflect their jeers. They'd hang their hands holding rosaries out the back windows of the car and yell at passersby, "Dear God, please help us! Our big sister is driving!" Through it all, Dad never looked up from his newspaper and sat unperturbed in the front passenger seat.

We didn't have seat belts in those days. We didn't even have seat belts when my children were little. I knew there was a danger, so I usually had my boys in the back seat. A generation later, I was putting my grandchildren in elaborate, protective car seats. I can't imagine driving today with kids in the back without making sure everyone was buckled in.

My senior year loomed, and I had no idea where I was going after high school. Wisconsin has several University of Wisconsin-affiliated colleges, and a couple of my teachers thought one of the state colleges might be in my reach. When I brought this up at home, no one was bowled over by my desire to go to college. My parents said that neighbors commented that going to the University of Wisconsin would turn me into a communist. My grandparents Anna and Anton said it might be worth sending boys to college but spending that kind of money on girls was not. I let their comments slide and followed my heart. I applied for scholarships and was offered one to Lawrence College, and I qualified for a University of Wisconsin tuition scholarship. I wanted to go to the biggest and furthest away one. I set my heart on going to the University of Wisconsin in

Madison. Dad said, "You want to go to college, don't you?" When I affirmed that, he said, "'I'll get a job making windows at Hurd Millwork. You will go to college."

I was going to college. It was going to happen. Here I was wearing my rebellious dungarees and about to become a communist at the University of Wisconsin. I couldn't believe my luck!

CHAPTER 22

Sarah and Franklin's Later Years

Franklin and Sarah with Great-Grandchildren

Mom and Dad retired from the farm in 1978, moved to Abbotsford, Wisconsin, and opened Sarah's Antiques. Mom found her greatest happiness and sense of pride in her business. Mom's store was in a three-car attached garage Dad added to a house they bought. They operated the shop until they retired in 1987.

Mom was a good businesswoman. My brother David remembers that she always knew how to bargain for what she wanted. When he was twelve or thirteen, Mom took him to Wausau to shop for a tweed overcoat that he had his eye on. He'd saved thirty-five dollars from results of his work trapping weasel, muskrat, and mink and selling pelts to Sears, Roebuck and Company. The coveted coat was sixty dollars and still beyond his means. Later that day, he met up with Mom and told her about the coat he liked but couldn't afford. Mom said, "Go back there and tell the salesclerk that you only have thirty-five dollars and see if he will sell it for that price." It had never occurred to David that people do that. When he went back and showed the shop owner all the money he had, lo and behold, the clerk said, "It's yours." My brother said that Mom teaching him that bargaining lesson has saved him a lot of money over his lifetime. It is no surprise to us that later in her life, Mom was able to use her innate business acumen to go into the antiques business.

Her interest in antiques started years earlier on the farm. She was creative and figured out how to use old farm objects left from the pioneering days of Dad's grandparents. She refinished an oxen yoke, and it became the holder of our mailbox. Geraniums filled copper tubs once used for heating water for bathing. Eventually, she started going to auctions and farm sales she'd seen in the newspapers to look for collectibles. The old things she found turned into wares that she priced dearly at Sarah's Antiques. She read books on antiques and collected furniture, dolls, jewelry, and art. We soon had six bedrooms of antiques including a brass bed that had been owned by nuns. One of the hollowed-out bedposts was full of children's uncorrected math papers.

The antiques business was interesting to both parents and provided supplemental income for them during their early retirement days. Dad learned to enjoy the business. He liked researching histories and prices of antiques and collectibles. Mom loved figuring out where the collectibles were and knowing how to spot finds and how to get in the targeted house to buy them. My son Steve remembers going to farms and crawling with her into musty, dirty attics and barns looking for furniture.

When I expressed an interest in art, Mom added that to her routine sales pitch. She would look for a driveway with grass growing in it because she said that old people without a car or who seldom drove lived there. She would go to the door and say that her daughter painted (I didn't) and that I was always looking for picture frames (I wasn't). Once she got in the house, nothing escaped her searching eyes. She usually walked out with a collectible item that would soon become a valuable antique. I was shocked by her brazenness.

Dad once sold a doll for a discounted price when he was tending the store. He said he felt sorry for the woman who was poor and wanted it for her daughter. Mom said, "I'm not in the business of giving away merchandise. Why, that woman will bring all her friends for cheap buys!" Toward the end of her life, she gave away the merchandise. She enjoyed giving the collectibles to her children. We all have gifts from Sarah's Antiques.

On her ninety-third birthday, I wrote a poem for her, which ended as follows:

I walk through my Florida House
and see the Loetz lamp and
Grandma's big black felt hat
Its stuffed blackbird with a broken wing
All the antiques you've given us
We will remember you even more for
Your soaring spirit, your great vigor
Your creativeness and persistence
You will always be with us.

Mom and Dad worked hard raising five kids and running a farm. Mom could outwork everyone, and she made sure there were no slackers. I sometimes think about how dogs will circle a spot before lying down. If we circled a chair, Mom quickly noticed and said, "There is something I want you to do…" There was no chance of sitting down. Lynda remembers when Mom was incapacitated due to back surgery. She made Lynda her maid. As Mom rested on the couch, she would point out dirt under the cupboard. "Man, did she have great eyesight! It's probably why I can spot dirt on the floor from ten feet away," Lynda commented. She mused, "I'm not certain if obsessive-compulsive disorder is hereditary, but my siblings and I think and act like we inherited this trait from Mom!"

Mom was quiet with a determined bossiness. It was a life-long habit. When she was 101, sitting in a rocking chair on the front porch of her Jacksonville, Florida, assisted care facility, she'd list things she wanted Barbara to pick up. She finished her instructions by saying, "Don't buy them at Walmart. They have shoddy stuff." Even Kleenex coming from Walmart she considered inferior to Kleenex sold in other stores.

Barbara and I winked at each other. The boss was still at it. She couldn't hear well, but she probably saw our wink exchange because she commented, "I guess I'm sounding bossy." I whispered to Barbara, "Hey, Mom, don't stop now!"

When she went to have her Wisconsin driving license renewed at ninety-five, she passed. She could drive for eight more years. However, she wasn't pleased with her photo, and she asked the clerk to take another; but he refused. I told her, "You should have taken the license and run before they realized how old you were."

Dad was a little more lenient than Mom. He taught us to be confident in ourselves by expecting the best from us. He required us to work hard, but he was less of a perfectionist. I learned to plow with the tractor when I was ten or eleven years old. This was difficult for me because the rows had to be straight and required me to look back a lot while driving. I wanted to make sure my lines were as straight as my dad's. It was all going well until I ran the tractor through a fence as I was checking if my furrow was straight. That's when the tears started, and I sat on top of that huge tractor sobbing over my mistake. I knew my dad wouldn't punish me for destroying the fence. The hot tears that rolled down my cheeks were over sheer embarrassment. I had failed. When Dad noticed, he walked out to the tractor to tell me not to worry and that he could fix the fence. Dad trusted us to handle situations and to do the right thing, but when things were beyond our control—like a tractor steering off course—he was always there.

When Barb and I were in our early teens, we'd babysit so Mom and Dad could go to dances where they'd gab with friends and waltz and polka the night away. Their love of spending the evening dancing continued until they were in their late seventies. In fact, for their fiftieth wedding anniversary, they had a big "come one, come all party." They had the invitation to their polka party printed in the local newspaper. My brothers and sisters and I were aghast at the open invitation. It was unheard of in our suburban lives.

"Do you want the whole town to show up?" we queried. They did, and the town obliged. More than two hundred people came. Church ladies prepared the food, and a polka band played at a community hall. With mixed drinks 1.50 dollars each at the open bar and church-lady food, their cost was minimal by our standards. My siblings and I came home for the party and watched Mom and Dad dance the night away. Long after we left that night, our parents continued to light up the dance floor. The next morning, they got up before we did and made us breakfast.

Sometimes they went to bars where much of rural social life took place. Even today, going to a supper club and stopping at bars to socialize on the way home is popular in parts of Wisconsin. Supper clubs are restaurants, Wisconsin-style, with free relish trays, crackers and cheese, and daily specials like fried chicken or perch. A favorite drink is a Brandy Old Fashioned. Bars as socialization venues may have been a carryover from the German tavern or beer hall, which, in immigrant days, was an integral part of community social life. Dad preferred grapefruit juice or a beer, but Mom liked a Brandy Old Fashioned. Wisconsin is right behind California in consumption of brandy with California's population being five times larger. Wisconsin is third in the nation in both number of bars and bars per capita. It must be the long cold winters. After Dad was deceased and Mom was still living on her own, she'd always ask us to take her to bars after we had dinner at Florena's

Supper Club in Medford. It was where she saw people she hadn't seen for a long time. I think my siblings complied and would hit three or four Medford bars after dinner. I did it once or twice but finally said one bar was enough for me.

Dad had a wry sense of humor and liked to tell jokes. In his old age, he lost his ability to type on his computer due to Parkinson's disease, but he could still forward a joke by hitting Send to his list. Mom didn't seem to have a sense of humor when we were young, and she seldom smiled. Something changed in her later years when she started antiquing. She livened up and even found her long lost sense of humor. She also seemed to relish the sole attention her eight years of widowhood gave her. At ninety-eight, she went to live with Barbara for eighteen months. They were sitting at a bar, waiting to be seated in a restaurant, when Barb said to the man seated next to her, "I'm here to find a date for my ninety-eight-year-old mother." Mom was hard of hearing, but she heard the comment and grumbled loudly for all to hear, "If you stopped telling people how old I am, I might find someone."

Other times, her humor was unintentional. An old friend asked her to come to visit him in his assisted living home in Wausau. He was also in his nineties and sometimes called to ask her to parties. Of course, Mom was going on ninety-eight and said the fifty-mile drive was too far since she was getting macular degeneration. Lynda said,

"Have your younger friend Susan drive you." Mom said, "Of course not. She'd steal him!"

Mom made up for her impoverished childhood by honing a taste for nice things. She projected a sense of aristocratic privilege, packaged with a beguiling smile loaded with expectations. She liked us taking care of her. One day, when she was in her nineties, we walked into her favorite clothing store, Chico's, and I found myself looking through the sale rack. "Hey, Mom, want to take a look at the sale rack?" She gave a disgusted look and said promptly, "If no one else wants them, why would I want them?" Princess Sarah. She would then give me her Chico order. "I'll take that outfit on the model—the sweater, the dress, the necklace—but I don't care for the bracelet." She often returned her purchases the next day and selected something else. She was finicky and not concerned about spending my money.

Sarah Ludwig Age 100

When Barbara and I took care of Mom in her last years, she gave orders and expected us to comply. Barbara was expected to visit her often at the assisted living facility and do her shopping. She was a saint for putting up with Mom. From me, she expected to get funds to live in a manner she wanted. I furnished the cash. My job was the easiest. She expressed her gratitude sincerely and regularly. She was charming most of the time.

Mom didn't like to talk about her childhood, and it was evident that she nursed hurts from growing up poor. When we asked if her parents spanked her, she said they hadn't, but other family members said her parents administered beatings. She was in her one-hundredth year when she said with chagrin that she never had a doll of her own and had to visit a neighbor girl so she could play with one. Her only dolls were paper ones she cut out of Sears, Roebuck and Company catalogs.

Mom's depression lasted until late in life. As I child, I resented her immense sadness, endless score-keeping, and bickering with neighbors and family. I thought she could will it away. I wanted to make her happier and thought if I were a better student or could win more awards, it would improve how she felt. I wasn't slavish about it. She obviously found me "sassy." She felt my disapproval. It was frustrating that nothing my brothers and sisters or I did could pierce her despondency.

I kept up my sunshine fairy routine for much of my life, only to realize it was not useful or healthy. It wasn't until trying to deal with an unhappy marriage that I learned more about myself through reading, therapy, and three years of graduate studies. It was almost a relief to learn that sad thoughts can't be willed away. I slowly forgave Mom and was able to appreciate her positive attributes. I passed on my wisdom to my sons. I said, "It's your job in your early adulthood to examine your childhood, determine what was good or bad about it, vow to raise your children with that knowledge, and, importantly, to forgive your parents. They did the best they could."

In her old age, she always had a worry du jour about someone in the family up until her death. She couldn't sleep well and agonized over problems. Yet when something serious happened, she recovered quickly. When I told her that her grandson, my son Greg, had terminal cancer at age forty-eight, she cried with me. The next day when I called her, she said, "Gramps [Dad] will be sitting in heaven doing his crossword puzzle when Greg comes, and he'll look up and say, 'What the hell are you doing here?'" We both laughed.

Dad was usually a calm person, but sometimes, he lost his temper. We knew he was mad when his voice rose, and he began with "Judas Priest." When he raised his voice, his children gave him their full attention.

Dad cared about small farms and mourned their loss. In his retirement years, he regretted the rise of factory farming that employed displaced farmers they'd put out of business. Some small farmers fought the spread of factory farms. They hated the large amount of animal waste, which often polluted the water table and nearby streams and created smells. The odors sometimes gave them respiratory problems like asthma. Many of the huge companies in the agribusiness were not even US companies. According to US Department of Agriculture Data, more than twenty-five million acres of US farmland is in the hands of foreign investors primarily in Canada, the Netherlands, and Germany, but also New Zealand, Saudi Arabia, and the United Arab Emirates.

State legislators tended to favor the agribusiness and passed laws favorable to their expansion. Dad wistfully remembered the Roosevelt years and wished that legislators had in mind the welfare of the small guy instead of implementing the wishes of agribusiness. Factory farms made a lot of money for their owners who were careful to keep on friendly terms with politicians. A few small farmers followed my dad's ideas of collectivizing their production for getting better prices. They have had some small successes but are fighting a losing battle. Too old to fight the end of family farms, he shook his head sadly. "Look at them," he said. "Look at the farmers who so prized their independence that they wouldn't get involved in collective bargaining. Where are they? If they haven't gone bankrupt or committed suicide, they are still on the family farms growing soybeans and corn for the factory farmers who are growing cattle as cheap as possible." In his heart, he felt that if small farmers had worked collectively to improve their economic situation, factory farms wouldn't have given the coup de grace to their livelihood.

Small farmers like Dad shield themselves from thinking about the short and brutal lives of animals. Dad unemotionally sent animals out for slaughter and slaughtered them on the farm. He long ago had numbed his feelings. It still seems more humane to have the life and death of these animals under the care of small farmers like Dad than under the watch of faceless corporations. How much easier it is for factory farms to crowd more animals in smaller spaces and cut back on their comfort and care. I eat meat two or three times a week and only rarely think about the animal's death. Like my dad, my feelings have been numbed. My feelings have been numbed, but not completely. I still miss my favorite cow, Rosie.

CHAPTER 23

Goodbye to the Farm

The Fritsche Homestead is no longer in the family. Mom and Dad sold it to neighbors in 1978. Two sisters have operated the farm in recent years. My siblings and I do not live in Wisconsin. We are scattered from coast to coast. Our memories of family and farm life live with us.

The farm was where I learned about death at an early age. Mom's philosophy about human deaths was practical: "We need to move on to make room for the next generation." Funerals were social occasions. In Dad's childhood, dead family members were laid out on the family dining room table on a black shawl. Neighbors brought food and often an envelope with five or ten dollars to help with funeral costs. Until she died, Mom put ten-dollar bills in envelopes to send to families she knew who had lost a loved one. Death was accepted as a natural part of life.

The farm is where my siblings and I learned the true meaning of hard work. It's not emptying waste baskets and setting the dining room table. Work on the farm often means dangerous and hot work, not giving up when thistles and dust cover your sweating body as you shove corn into the maw of the blower that sends chopped corn into the silo and whose blades could kill you. There are no days off for farming, no vacation days, and no time and a half for overtime. It is a twenty-four-seven job.

We learned the value of money. We didn't have much. A quarter was a lot of money to kids in the 1950s. We learned to be frugal and save money. We tried to pull our own weight and help the family thrive. I worked twenty hours a week and summers through college and paid most of my own way. My brothers and sisters helped put themselves through college. We were grateful to our parents who supported us through college, although it meant adding more work to their already long hard days.

We learned to take care of and look out for one another because we were important cogs in a family business. Every family member was needed in this labor-intensive business, and little fights and arguments deterred us from being productive.

We learned from our parents that we needed to take care of the land. They taught us the principles of conservation.

Rotating crops helps keep the soil rich and plants healthy. Each crop affects the soil in different ways, so a field planted in corn one year might be planted in alfalfa the next. Dad taught us how to prevent soil erosion by plowing around hills rather than up and down. He spread manure over tilled fields with a tractor and manure spreader to enrich the soil. If we did not take care of the land, it would not take care of us.

We learned to appreciate and take care of what we had. We learned how to grow foods, take care of animals, and take care of property. We knew how to change a tire, fix a fence, paint a farm building, and launder, sew, mend, and iron our own clothing. Sometimes fixing something or living with the imperfect was embarrassing as one of my brothers remembers going to college with holes in the soles of his shoes.

We learned to appreciate the hard work that goes into putting food on our tables. As a farm family, we knew that the colorful and bountiful vegetables and fruit in grocery stores, the exotic and familiar meat, and brown and white eggs displayed there did not fall from the sky. We knew firsthand that many people work hard sowing and reaping crops, feeding and growing and butchering animals, trucking the products, and displaying and selling food in our grocery stores. Our parents tried to make us eat anything we put on our plates. It taught us to take only what we could eat.

Sarah and Franklin's grandchildren grew up respecting their grandparents and learning from them as we did. Son Steve wrote to his grandfather in his last year about his memories of the farm:

May 2008

Dear Gramps,

I hope you are content. I hope that, toward the end of my years, I can look back on a life spent something like yours because you have been best among men. Your vision has been clear, your heart compassionate, and your soul honest. For me, your love and integrity were never alloyed.

When I was thirteen, you brought me to your farm in Wisconsin to help you bring the hay in. Not much help but some. I remember mostly raking hay in the afternoon and spreading feed for the cows when they were milked in the evening. I was mad about guns and you lent me a BB gun that I used to shoot at and miss small birds.

One evening that summer, I did something terrible. Bringing the cows in from the fields in ninety-degree heat, I ran your dog Princess after the cows to hurry them home. I really should have known better, but there you are. Fortunately, none of them went down. Not so lucky for Princess. Having been encouraged to do this once, she could be depended on to do it again. You sent Uncle Lin into the woods to shoot her. I tagged along. I was less interested in shooting birds after that. I still feel bad about that dog. Thank you for allowing me to learn by making mistakes. Thank you for forgiving me that and any other trials I put you through that summer. I will always remember that summer fondly.

When I was fourteen, I came up for haying and you put me on the back of a wagon. I was about 132 pounds but strong. Still, I had never really been asked to do a man's work before. I remember my nose filled with hay dust and thistles lined my clothes. I remember being soaked with sweat and dizzy from the heat. I thought more of it at the time than you did. All boys start thus on a farm. But you knew I came from a soft life and so you were patient and encouraged me. Thank you for that. Through you, I learned that I could almost do a man's work, and so I felt that I could become a man.

With great love and respect,
Your grandson Steve

Jeff, my middle son, wrote about his experiences on the farm:

June 25, 2019

The farm was an explosion of exotic sights, sounds, and smells to a kid from the suburbs of Chicago. Those exotic smells and sights were the same over time, but through the eyes of a boy, and through the eyes of a teenager were somehow differ-ent. The one constant, though, through all those years was the watchful eye of a loving Grandma and the stern but loving teacher Gramps.

I can recall the intoxicating smell of cocoa wafting through the house on cold winter mornings, malted milk in the summer, fresh doughnuts just out of the fryer, and chocolate chip cookies in a jar that seemed to be on auto-refill. I loved the mysterious rooms in the old farmhouse and exploring the curious buildings on the property—chicken coops, the pig house, equipment shed, and of course the barn where we played hide-and-seek in the haymow.

As a teenager, the same stimuli was there, but they took a back seat to observing things like the marvel of the milk system in the barn. Working every day to help Gramps do the milking you'd see the huge stainless-steel tanks in the milk room fill within two to three days and then emptied out by the milk truck—only for the process to start again. The smell of lime disinfectant was ever present after the morning milking. As a teenager, the new stimuli was beginning to connect the sights and sounds of the farm to something totally new. It was a business. Work in > milk out, with a little antique business on the side. Work was measured in watts and ergs (even if those terms were not used).

My most formative experience on
the farm happened one summer during
hay season. I normally worked with my
older brother Steve, but for some reason
he was not present. I was a scrawny twelve
or thirteen-year-old who was too small
to work in the back of the bailer stacking
hay on the wagon as it went through the
fields. That was tough work—a man's job.
However, that summer I was old enough
to run filled wagons back to the barn,
crank up the bale elevator, and offload
the sixty-pound bales onto the elevator.
When the wagon was empty, I went up
into the haymow where it was a hundred
degrees and restacked the bales in twenty
rows that were five feet high. They would
be salted and used as the main source of
food for the cows during the cold, long
Wisconsin winters. In prior years, I was
relegated to the job of raking, which was
still kind of cool for a young kid from the
suburbs. I loved driving the big old tractor. So, this year I finally got to do some
of the hard work.

At the end of summer, we went into
town one Saturday afternoon for the trac-

tor pulls. I can recall an electric buzz of activity in town that afternoon. Medford was a small farm town, but on a Saturday afternoon as the hay season approached its end, even as a kid you could feel the need for people to socialize, connect, and relax. That day, Grandma and Gramps made a stop at the local tavern. Gramps had his usual beer and Grandma her Brandy Old Fashioned. I was satisfied playing pinball by myself in the corner. After about twenty minutes, Gramps walked over to me with a fresh draft beer and said, "You've done a man's work this week." He put down the beer on the pinball machine and returned to his seat. Not a man of many words, but a man who chose his words wisely.

Greg, my youngest son, remembered his summer on the farm:

June 2008

Hi, Gramps,

I have always been proud of you and Grandma because you were farmers (and your children who were farmers as kids).

Today, the world is so much about greed, money, and material things. I love the fact that my mom grew up on a working dairy farm. It makes me feel more grounded in life.

You and Grandma set a good example for my mom about hard work and being compassionate. I hope it's fair to say that my mom in turn passed on these qualities to me. As you know, I have been successful in business. The example you set for my mom and that she in turn set for me is a big part of my success. Her passion to help people in her non-profit work also rubbed off on me which is why today I now spend most of my time on three non-profits I opened to help homeless men and women get back to work and reenter mainstream society. So, I just wanted you to know that you and Grandma (and my mom through your example) have had a huge effect on the person I am today.

Visits to the farm: I remember sleeping on the velvet blue couch in your living room when visiting which was just outside your and Grandma's bedroom. One time when we were visiting for Christmas, Jeff and I built a huge snow fort in the front yard. My brother, Steve, took an ax and smashed it up. I was so mad that I took an iron toy tractor Grandma bought me at the five and dime and threw it at his head. I'm glad I missed, but boy were you mad. Since I was always fighting with my older brothers, you used to call me "Toughie."

I also remember playing in the hay loft. I can still recall the smell of the new hay. I remember you letting me steer the tractor while I sat in your lap. I used to love to play in the huge shed where you stored your antiques. There were so many neat things in there.

Finally, I have always enjoyed your sense of humor. Sixteen years ago, I called you and Grandma to tell you I was going to get married. You said you probably would not make it to my wedding and that you did not buy green bananas any-more. I imagine I will say the same thing once I am a Grandpa. Another saying you always use when I ask you how you're doing is "Some days chickens, some days feathers." I use this a lot when people ask me the same thing. A lot of people don't understand since they've never been on a farm, but I say it because it reminds me of you.

Gramps, I want you to know that I am thinking of you and Grandma and that your grandson loves you both very much.

Your Grandson, Greg Block

Nina, my brother Dave's oldest child, wrote to Grandma Sarah on her one-hundredth birthday:

We stepped into another world when we visited Grandma and Grandpa, whether they were living at the farm or later when they lived on Main Street in Abbotsford. I was fascinated by the farm and what happened in the barn and outdoors. The driveway to the farmhouse seemed a mile long. It was bordered by a huge garden and lined with the pine trees my father planted as a child. The way the house was run and the things that needed to be done were often different from my home. The third thing that amazed me was all the stuff!

The barn and outdoor activities were very different for female grandchildren than it was for our male cousins in the 1960s and 1970s. We did not attend "hay baling summer camp" like the boys did! My memories include the magic (and horror) of seeing a calf born and hoping I never had to come within ten feet of a nasty barn cat. Grandma said I could bring my friend, Jane, along on one trip, and we entertained ourselves by trying to get the cows to run by throwing rocks at them. This elicited an angry reaction from Grandpa which is something my male cousins can relate to.

My favorite memories include making huge snow forts that did not cave in and visiting the abandoned schoolhouse that my dad and his siblings attended. We visited the one room school as recently as 2008, or just before Grandma moved to Florida to live with Aunt Barbara. Mostly, I recall walking around the property, avoiding Princess the dog (she was mean), getting water out of the old well pump, kicking rocks and not watching television.

Many of my most treasured memories are of being inside with Grandma and Grandpa. Visiting always included Grandma's made-from-scratch doughnuts—fresh, soft, and warm—and heavily sugared. When Grandpa was younger, he smoked his pipes in the den while he watched a very small black-and-white television. We had dinners that were almost as big as our lunches. Hot beef sandwiches, beef roast, and ham were common.

On special occasions we spoke with relatives on the telephone (attached to the wall, of course), and often had to make sure no one was already speaking on the party line, a less expensive phone service with one shared line. We had to pick up the phone and listen for anyone else speaking. A lot of gossip probably traveled through the party line.

When I was a very little girl, Grandma was building her antiques business, and we arrived to find new treasures she found. They built the pole barn to house Grandma's antique shop, and it was like a museum. I distinctly remember the antique U-shaped bar and the dressed-up mannequins. We loved to walk around and look, especially up in the attic! Grandma and Grandpa taught me how to respect other people's belongings. They trusted us to visit their shop... I do not recall if I ever broke something.

After playing outside, we took a bath before bedtime. The water did not have a controlled thermostat—it was hotter than any water I have ever felt. When we were small enough, we thought it was fun to sleep on two large, soft, comfy armchairs that were pushed together in the living room. When we got a little older, we slept in the big Victorian beds that I coveted. They were only full-size mattresses, but we thought they were enormous because of the tall, stylized headboards. I am blessed to have one of those bedroom sets in my own home now. I treasure it.

Once I was married and had my own children in the 1990s, my husband and

I visited Grandma and Grandpa at their home in Abbotsford. My husband and I often stayed at the Home Motel, not that it was especially comfortable or nice, but one of us could easily walk back and forth so our baby/toddler daughters could nap. We were there to celebrate the big auction when many antiques were sold off.

After Grandpa passed away, I always enjoyed sitting in the evening with Grandma. The girls were in their sleeping bags in the sunroom. She was not a big drinker but was interested in talking and having a couple of glasses of wine at the kitchen table before we went to bed. In the morning, she always had a coffee cake and a pound of bacon cooked before anyone else woke up.

I treasure the memories that I can pass on to my children, but I also treasure another gift my Grandparents passed on: I appreciate old things. I like mixing old things and antiques with the new and modern. They had an antique pharmacy back/counter and all sorts of antiques. Flow blue pottery was one of Grandma's passions, along with all sorts of depression glass. I coveted some from the time I was a child and am fortunate to have a few of them now.

Love, Nina Fiedler

Dad and Mom lived in their house in Abbotsford for thirty years after selling the family farm, but eventually, we had to move Dad into an assisted living facility. I knew Dad was failing when he couldn't fill out a simple medical form and asked for my help. I looked at his checkbook, and tiny, crooked handwriting had replaced the graceful script he once had. He had been falling, breaking bones, and had developed a frozen stare, indicators of Parkinson's disease.

When a pianist played his favorite tunes in his assisted living home, I would dance with him in his wheelchair. He loved listening to music until his death. He remembered every word of old songs and sang along like he did when we drove in the car so long ago. In the last year of his life, he was finally given a diagnosis of Parkinson's disease with Lewy Body Disease. Dad died of a stroke at his assisted living home in Abbotsford, Wisconsin, on December 10, 2008. He was ninety-three.

Mom's mind didn't seem touched by her age, and she was sharp up until the last couple of weeks of her life. She chose her assisted living place when she was one-hundred years old. When she moved in, I made her pay for the first two months from her Social Security savings. I knew she would walk away in a few days if it were my money. She did a tryout in another assisted living residence that I paid for and walked out after two days, calling it a prison. She adjusted well on her second try. I whispered to the director, "Mom is a hundred. Is she the oldest resident?" The director responded, "There are eighty-year-olds here that are older than your mom."

Within the first weeks at what turned out to be her final home, she had herself moved three times until she found the exact room she wanted on the first floor with large windows and close to the dining room. She managed to accomplish that with a smile, grace, and steely resolve. She didn't give up her taste for nice things. She saw a fellow resident at lunch who had a fancy walker and tried to convince me to buy her the same one-thousand-dollar walker. I resisted. She upped the sales pitch. "It could be an heirloom to pass down to family members. You will all need it someday." She had a perfectly fine walker, and I denied the request but found her sales pitch amusing.

She celebrated her one-hundredth birthday in Florida, where we owned a house. It was held at our club with a grand gathering of family. A year later, she had a more subdued one-hundred-first birthday gathering of a few family members at the assisted living residence. She was failing.

I wrote about her at that time:

One hundred and one years
Almost blind
Almost deaf
A fierce grip on her walker
Life is ebbing
A strong spirit holds on.

Mom died at age 101. Her official cause of death was colon cancer. She had been cycling in and out of the hospital for atrial fibrillation (A-fib), congestive heart failure, and colon cancer. She was almost blind and deaf. A couple of weeks before she passed, she told me she planned to refuse all medications except fiber to prevent blockage. She told her doctor she didn't want any new interventions and that she was ready for hospice. She refused an oxygen tank. She said, "I've scheduled a manicure/pedicure for next Monday. I will put lots of salt on my food and have a Brandy Old Fashioned. I'll leave after that." She died peacefully in hospice care at her assisted living facility on April 22, 2017. The tough lady we call Mom retained a sense of humor until the end. We will all have to walk our own paths to death. I hope I do as well.

CHAPTER 24

October 7, 2016—Eighty Years Old

Ludwig children: Lin, Barbara, Lynda, Nadine, David

It's my eightieth birthday. I can't believe I'm that old. I feel twenty years younger. I'm sipping a margarita on a patio sofa under a shade umbrella and listening to a mariachi band. It's late afternoon, humid, and a sunny eighty-five degrees. I can see the surf and hear its roar. Most of the family is out sportfishing but will be back shortly. The rest are in their villas, dressing for the birthday dinner. My son

Jeff and his wife, Karen, own this beautiful beachside estate in Puerto Escondido, Mexico; they are hosting me and my siblings and their spouses for my birthday bash. How lucky I am to be alive and healthy in this beautiful place surrounded by people I love. The little girl who wanted to escape the Wisconsin dairy farm did just that. It has been a great journey!

My husband, a semi-retired attorney in his mid-eighties, is not here. He seldom travels now as he isn't well. He has become a grumpy-but-mostly lovable old guy with lung disease and heart problems brought on by age and smoking. He is unable or unwilling to walk in airports and refuses to take a handicapped cart. Driving a car allows him to roll down the windows and enjoy his favorite activity, smoking. He drives without a seat belt as he says, "The government is not going to tell me what to do." He couldn't drive to Mexico, so he's not here. Bill and I have been married for eighteen years. We married a couple of years after Jared Block and I divorced in 1996.

Jared and I were married for thirty-two years. We have three children: Steven, living in Belvedere, California, with his wife, Dana; Jeff, living in San Francisco, California, with his wife, Karen; and Greg, living in Atlanta, Georgia, with his wife, Monica. I have seven grandchildren from my marriage to Jared and three step-grandchildren with Bill.

During my senior year at The University of Wisconsin where I was studying to be a teacher, I was in Beloit on a teaching internship from UW. That's where I met Jared. He was from Janesville, Wisconsin, and was attending Milton College. He was handsome and exciting and said he would be a millionaire before he was thirty. It was a difficult marriage from the beginning. He had fourteen jobs in the first ten years we were married. I had never experienced such instability. He seemed unable to work for anyone, but if he got fired or quit, he had a better-paying job the next day. He was an enigma. He was driven to be successful and could sell anything to anybody. He sold me! And yes, he was almost a millionaire before he was thirty. It took him until the age thirty-five.

While it was often an unhappy marriage, I decided that I had made my bed and would lie in it. I would get an advanced degree and put money from my work into funds for my children's education. I started graduate school when my youngest son went to kindergarten, and I spent three years at The Ohio State University studying school psychology. I started working as a school psychologist in 1975. I enjoyed the work and felt like I could contribute to education. I was asked to take over the state school psychology association lobbyist position a few years later. It was a part-time job, so I spent half of my time in schools and half at the state legislature. In 1987, I founded the Center for Effective Discipline, a nonprofit, to educate the public on the effects of corporal punishment in schools and alternatives to its use. In 1993, I started working full-time on the effort to end corporal punishment in Ohio public schools. I was committed to that goal, and, stubborn German that I am, I did not quit until it was banned in Ohio Public Schools in 2009.

Our family's financial situation became infinitely better in the mid-1980s. Jared hit pay dirt when we founded what became a multimillion-dollar company, American Pacific Enterprises, that imported textiles from China. He already had a profitable business representing textile mills but decided that he needed to begin importing as US textile mills were dying. He created excitement in his import business, but his entrepreneurial bent often had him in court, responding to lawsuits. More drama.

The year before he died having pancreatic cancer, he was diagnosed with a type of depression. With medication, family members said Jared lived a happier last year. Looking back, the bravado and creativity that gave him an edge in business were probably symptoms of the disease he'd suffered from for years. I never had a dull day in my marriage, not that I didn't yearn for a few.

The divorce settlement left me with funds to live comfortably. Jared retired before the divorce and left our sons in charge of the business. I went on to travel, take up art, and write. I have visited sixty-five countries and see no end to travel in sight. I have many happy memories.

The fishing crowd has returned and awakened me from my memories. Joining me on the patio is my sister Barbara Schmidt and her boyfriend, John; my sister Lynda Long and her husband, Dave; and my brother Lin and his girlfriend, GiGi. The mariachi band is enjoying the crowd, and happy voices raise the noise level. Jeff comes out to lead everyone into the dining room for the birthday dinner. The setting glows. All the beachside doors have been pulled back, so we are virtually outdoors, steps from the beach and the pounding surf. Beautiful cut tropical flowers give off a sweet fragrance. More wine flows, more toasts are made.

As we finish our dessert, Jeff calls me to join him on the patio in view of the seated guests. Off to the side is a large Trump piñata. He hands me a wooden bat and ties a dark napkin over my eyes. "Go to it, Mom! I know this will be fun for you!" I take a mighty swing and feel the wrapped candy innards of the piñata falling around me. I keep swinging until I am breathless. Jeff was right. I did enjoy his special surprise.

I thanked my son and daughter-in-law for their hospitality. As we wended our way back to our rooms, I called my brothers and sisters for a peek out of the kitchen window at a pile of liquor and wine bottles from the party.

It looked like a fraternity house on Sunday morning. We exchanged hugs and laughingly said we should go to rehab when we get home. My beautiful eightieth birthday party has come to an end.

EPILOGUE

Twelve years ago, I published *Our Family: Wisconsin Pioneers, Stories for My Grandchildren*, a picture book with short biographies of ancestors. Young members of the family found the book useful for their "family tree" school projects. Since the book was such a success, I began to harbor the idea of writing about the life of our immediate family on the Fritsche Homestead founded by our great grandparents in the late 1880's.

Remembering Rosie, a story about mid-twentieth century Wisconsin farm life, arose from memories of children and grandchildren of Sarah and Franklin Ludwig. Memories are a blend of fact and fiction. Ours are the same. Chapter 3, which introduces the Ludwig family in 1950, is my memory of the way our family interacted at that time, rather than an exact story of that day.

Over five years, my siblings and I exchanged e-mails and tried to sharpen and coalesce our memories. We made use of memories of old neighbors and family friends. Sibling reunions elicited new family memories. At a 2018 reunion in Maui, we combined a lovely vacation with evening "memory sessions." "I can beat that story" was a frequent segue into more memories.

Many of them tickled us, and some will go forever unrepeated. The book provides for our grandchildren a history of their Wisconsin family—how our immigrant ancestors lived their lives, how our family adapted to changing farming practices and economic actualities over time, and how we bonded in a shared identity that began with the Fritsche Homestead in the late 1880s.

The purpose of the book is not to eulogize the American family dairy farm, which has almost disappeared. It is not intended to provide an example of an exemplary immigrant farm family. It is an ordinary family with no great writers, poets, artists, professors, physicians, engineers, or politicians. It is a family with ordinary interpersonal tensions, and a family that experienced small successes and, fortunately, no calamities. An ordinary American rural family of the mid-twentieth century. It is a family that genuinely enjoys being together and works hard to maintain a loving relationship. Perhaps that is its greatest accomplishment.

ACKNOWLEDGMENTS

Thanks to those who provided information for this book.

Steve, Jeff, and Greg Block and Nina Fidler, Sarah and Franklin's grandchildren shared their memories of the family farm. Their perspectives show how farm experiences with loving families, even in small doses, shape lives of children.

Sharon Connell, Chippewa Falls, Wisconsin, provided information about the Joseph Fritsche family in a private publication, *The Lifeline of Joseph Fritsche*, for years 1847 to present (no date).

Sigita Toleikiene and family members living in Lithuania supplemented our mother's information about the Milles family when my sister Barbara and I visited them in 2003.

Brenda Ludwig, a Canadian cousin, provided well-documented research on the Ludwig family in Germany and the US.

The following publications awakened my interest and memories and increased my knowledge of farm life in Taylor County, Wisconsin.

Log Cabin News of the Taylor County Historical Society, Germans in Wisconsin by the State Historical Society of Wisconsin, and *Images of America: Taylor County* by Robert P. Rusch.

Thank you to those who helped me with editing.

Karen Vujnovic went beyond copyediting. She addressed my writing style weaknesses and helped me find my voice.

Linda Sexton, a developmental editor, valiantly tried to drag me from a writing style honed by my work as a school psychologist and a lobbyist for nonprofits to a more creative style.

Together, they helped me improve this nostalgia memoir. I am forever grateful.

SOURCES

Chapter 2

Childbirth in the Mid-Twentieth Century Including Percentage of Women Giving Birth at Home

"A General Overview of Significant Events in the History of Childbirth in America Over the Past 300 Years." https://sites.google.com/site/historyofchildbirthinamerica/historical-resources/historical-timeline.

http://momotics.com/events-in-the-history-of-childbirth/.

Wertz, Richard W., Dorothy C. Wertz. *Lying-In: A History of Childbirth in America.* Yale University Press, 1989.

Chapter 4

Make-up of Downtown Medford, Wisconsin, in the Late 1880s

"The Early History of Medford, Wisconsin," https://sites.rootsweb.com/~witaylor/histories/earlyhistory.htm.

The information from Ancestry.com is an early history (1876) of Taylor County, Wisconsin, as found in the records of the Wisconsin Land Commission and was copied November 5, 1937, by the Assistant Secretary of the Land Commission.

Food Prices in 1880s

Centennial Committee. "100-Year Anniversary 1874–1974." Stetsonville Little Black Deer Creek.

In Author's Archives.

Chapter 5

The Number of Germans Who Came to Wisconsin at the Time of the Immigration of Our Grandparents

Richard H. Zeitlin, *Germans in Wisconsin*. The State Historical Society of Wisconsin Madison, 1977, 3.

Chapter 7

The Percentage of Households with Electricity

TheHistoricalArchive,https://www.thehistoricalarchive.com/happenings/57/the-history-of-electricity-a-timeline/.

Chapter 8

The Number of Lithuanian Immigrants and How They Were Designated by Ethnicity

Balys J. P. "The American Lithuanian Press." *Lithuanian Quarterly Journal of Arts and Sciences* 22, no. 1 (Spring 1976). The Library of Congress. http://www.lituanus. org/1976/76_1_02.htm.

Chapter 18

Medical Costs in Mid-Twentieth Century, Medford, Wisconsin

Berglund, Mark. "Early Medical History of Medford, Wisconsin," *The Star News,* Medford, Wisconsin, April 2, 2009.

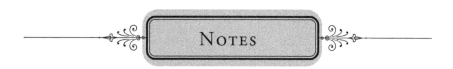

Notes

Where are the Ludwig siblings today?

Barbara

Barbara is the second oldest child. She has lived in Jacksonville, Florida, for almost fifty years. She married Charles (Chuck) Schmidt after he graduated from The University of Wisconsin in La Crosse, where they met. Barbara became a registered medical technologist and later, a real estate agent. Chuck worked for many years as a salesman for IBM. After his retirement, they separated and still live apart. Barbara remains in the family condominium on the Intracoastal in Jacksonville. Two daughters, Carey (Keven Bowles) and Lisa (Tom Snead), live in Jacksonville, and each has two children. Jake Snead and his wife, Elizabeth, made Barbara and Chuck great-grandparents with a son, Austin, in April 2019. Barbara—still a pretty, lively blond lady of eighty-something—finds it soul-rending that she has a daughter who is a grandmother.

Lynda

Lynda, the youngest girl, attended The University of Wisconsin, Eau Claire, where she met and married David Long. For a time, they lived in Michigan, where David taught school. They moved to Ohio in 1980, and David and Lynda both worked for a time for American Pacific Enterprises. Lynda later became a successful real estate agent in Ohio and served as the president of the Columbus Board of Realtors and held other board-elected and appointed positions. They have two adult children, Tina and Jason.

David

David, the middle child and oldest son, retired as senior vice president of WellPoint Insurance (now Anthem) in California. His wife, Rebecca, was an executive vice president of the company. They both retired in 2000, but after a year of retirement, she went back to work as CEO of two WellPoint companies, Blue Cross Blue Shield of Georgia and Blue Cross Blue Shield of Wisconsin, finally retiring for the second time in 2005. They have homes in Maui and Santa Barbara, California. Dave has three children living in Milwaukee by his first marriage to Carole Carlson: Nina Fiedler (Bob), Amy Kubinski, and Andy Ludwig (Theresa). They have five grandchildren.

Lin

Lin Ludwig (Serpil, deceased) lives in Fort Myers, Florida, and is a real estate agent. For many years, he worked for American Pacific Enterprises. The baby of the family, he has two children in Los Angeles: Linzey (Garrett Strommen) and Brittany Ludwig. Linzey and Garrett have two towheaded preschoolers, Miller and Luna.

ABOUT THE AUTHOR

Nadine A. Block has ceaselessly and successfully fought for children's rights for three decades. She was a teacher, a school psychologist, and the founder and director of a non-profit organization that fought to end school corporal punishment. Block previously published *This Hurts Me More Than It Hurts You: Children Share in Words and Pictures How Spanking Hurts and What to Do Instead* (2011) and *Breaking the Paddle: Ending School Corporal Punishment* (2013). During her retirement, she privately published *Our Family: Wisconsin Pioneers, Stories for My Grandchildren* and other stories for her grandchildren, using personal travel photos and illustrations, including "Casey the Cat in Kathmandu" and "Corey the Camel in Timbuktu."

CPSIA information can be obtained
at www.ICGtesting.com
Printed in the USA
BVHW030538100921
616495BV00007B/2

9 781662 430503